METHODOLOGY
OF THE
BEHAVIORAL SCIENCES

Publication Number 597

AMERICAN LECTURE SERIES®

A Monograph in

The BANNERSTONE DIVISION *of*
AMERICAN LECTURES IN PHILOSOPHY

Edited By

MARVIN FARBER, Ph.D.
Department of Philosophy
State University of New York at Buffalo

METHODOLOGY
of the
BEHAVIORAL SCIENCES

Problems and Controversies

By

ROLLO HANDY

State University of New York at Buffalo

CHARLES C THOMAS • PUBLISHER

Springfield • Illinois • U.S.A.

Published and Distributed Throughout the World by

CHARLES C THOMAS • PUBLISHER

BANNERSTONE HOUSE
301-327 East Lawrence Avenue, Springfield, Illinois, U.S.A.

NATCHEZ PLANTATION HOUSE
735 North Atlantic Boulevard, Fort Lauderdale, Florida, U.S.A.

© *1964, by* CHARLES C THOMAS • PUBLISHER

Library of Congress Catalog Card Number: 64-22070

With THOMAS BOOKS careful attention is given to all details of manufacturing and design. It is the Publisher's desire to present books that are satisfactory as to their physical qualities and artistic possibilities and appropriate for their particular use. THOMAS BOOKS will be true to those laws of quality that assure a good name and good will.

Printed in the United States of America
S–4

To Toni, Jon, and Ellen

PREFACE

PRACTICING scientists sometimes say that philosophers writing on the methodology of the behavioral sciences do not show the necessary familiarity with actual scientific work, or do not discuss the problems that are most significant. Even if scientists are not correct about such matters, there seems to be a place for a book putting primary emphasis on methodological issues that are regarded as important by scientists and that arise in many of the behaviorial disciplines.

My concern with the problems discussed in this book goes back to a seminar in methodology taught many years ago by Marvin Farber. I hope I have profited from his insistence on avoiding the obscurantism and near mysticism that sometimes pervade discussions of the topic. The writings of C. West Churchman and Mario Bunge have also influenced me considerably. Discussions with the officers of the Behavioral Research Council, E. C. Harwood, George Lundberg, and Stuart C. Dodd, have also been stimulating. Since all those mentioned no doubt would disagree strongly with some of the things I have said, my interest in their work in no sense is to be construed as agreement in points of view.

It is a pleasure to thank The Research Foundation of State University of New York for a fellowship, and The Committee on the Allocation of Research Funds of the State University of New York at Buffalo for a grant, both of which were helpful in the completion of the manuscript at this time.

Finally, I want to express my appreciation to the Behavioral Research Council for permission to adapt for this volume some of the materials and examples used in Rollo Handy and Paul Kurtz, *A Current Appraisal of the Behavioral Sciences* (Behavioral Research Council, Great Barrington, Massachusetts, 1964).

R.H.

CONTENTS

METHODOLOGY
OF THE
BEHAVIORAL SCIENCES

1

INTRODUCTION

1. RELATION OF PHILOSOPHERS AND SCIENTISTS

MANY conflicting accounts of the proper or desirable relation of philosophic to scientific inquiry can be found. Although we are frequently told that the philosopher's major task is to analyze, clarify, elucidate, or otherwise inquire into the language used by working scientists, the philosophic scene still contains those offering prescriptions (overt or implied) of what scientists ought to do. For example, what scientists are inclined to regard as empirical questions to be settled by scientific means are sometimes considered by philosophers as "logical" or "conceptual" questions to be settled by some form of language analysis.[1] Philosophic accounts of how scientists supposedly proceed, or should proceed, fill many pages of the learned journals and help to raise the level of book production, although the impact of such philosophic aid on scientific practice is often slight.

Judging by the articles and books on philosophy of science written in the last decade, philosophers often begin with some notion of the best way to philosophize, and then apply that notion to their analyses of scientific work. One cannot read far without encountering admonitions that we should pay attention to what scientists do, rather than to what they say; but the descriptions given of what scientists do are often interesting reflections of the describer's philosophic predilections. Logical Positivists thus put much emphasis on protocol sentences; recently Wittgensteinian

---

[1] For a recent attempt to show that social scientists often make the mistake of regarding as empirical questions what are *a priori* conceptual questions, see Peter Winch: *The Idea of a Social Science and Its Relation to Philosophy*, London, Routledge & Kegan Paul, 1958. For a witty counter to this type of view, see John H. Randall, Jr.: Talking and looking, *Proceedings and Addresses of the American Philosophical Association, 1956-1957*, Yellow Springs, Ohio, 1957. Randall maintains that philosophers often do too much talking and not enough looking.

understanding has been given quite a play; and in some circles traditional Idealistic theses are stressed in accounts of scientific endeavors; etc.

If working scientists typically exhibited great talent in clearly and adequately analyzing the methods they use, philosophers probably could leave philosophy of science alone. But unfortunately the most successful users of a method are sometimes inept in their attempts to describe it. Often this stems from a great desire to get on with the inquiry itself, combined with a lack of training or practice in the requisite analytic skills. Philosophers' professional interests, education, and characteristic ways of approaching tasks may make them helpful commentators on scientific methodology.

For present purposes, the major (but not the only) task of philosophers is taken as inquiry into inquiry.[2] The view here is that the labels "science" and "scientific" have been used variously and inconsistently, and hence decisions must be made as to the application of those terms. The rise of modern science has been characterized by many successful inquiries commonly designated "scientific." An analysis of those inquiries and the reasons for their success, as compared to other modes of approach, yields what in this essay is taken as descriptive of scientific inquiry. Since some of the greatest scientists may cast their results in language stemming from philosophic, religious, and ideological convictions, skepticism is often called for in accepting verbal accounts of what has been done. In principle, however, the investigative behavior of scientists should be open to objective observation.

2. SCOPE OF BOOK

Some topics discussed in the recent literature on the philosophy of science are generated more by certain ways of philosophizing than from the actual practices of scientists. This may account for

---

[2]The phrase is taken from a collection of essays by Arthur F. Bentley: *Inquiry Into Inquiries: Essays in Social Theory*, Sidney Ratner, ed., Boston, Beacon Press, 1954. Bentley's comments are either neglected or maligned by most philosophers; his pungent and irreverent views deserve close consideration. Perhaps his methodological views will eventually become as successful as his *The Process of Government*, Chicago, University of Chicago Press, 1908. This volume had little, if any, effect on his contemporaries interested in political science, but some twenty years later it began to be influential and now is frequently referred to as a classic.

the relative indifference of so many scientists to the alleged clarifications tendered by philosophers. With some frequency scientists say that the views on science held by philosophers simply could not be held by anyone thoroughly familiar with the relevant scientific activities.[3] On the other hand, there seems to be no reason for assuming that the philosophy of science literature produced by scientists will always be helpful in an inquiry into scientific inquiry. For present purposes, it is hoped that at least some progress may be made if major, but not exclusive, emphasis is put on those controversies, problems, and difficulties that the scientists themselves have discussed in recent years. Although it may seem unwise for a philosopher to focus on the writings of scientists, and although doubtless any philosopher will go seriously astray in assessing some of that work, it seems even more dangerous for a philosopher to write on the methodology of the behavioral sciences without first undergoing a thorough immersion in the activities of those scientists.

The present volume was written after a fairly intensive survey of the behavioral science literature of approximately the last ten years.[4] One conclusion was that workers in some disciplines are much concerned about issues that are discussed only rarely or not at all by people from other disciplines. When common problems can be found, the terminology often differs to an extreme degree from discipline to discipline. In some fields the battle lines are clearly drawn, the arguments nicely assembled, and the rejoinders neatly put together. In other fields the same controversies occur in a more primitive and less clear way. And on occasion just the controversy that one would expect to find emphasized in a particular discipline seems to be discussed there hardly at all.

---

[3]See, for example, the criticism of Max Black, made by Talcott Parsons in Max Black, ed.: *The Social Theories of Talcott Parsons: A Critical Examination*, Englewood Cliffs, N. J., Prentice-Hall, 1961, pp. 340-341. This is not to say that Parsons is necessarily correct, but rather to illustrate the failure of communication between philosophers and scientists. Also of interest is the criticism of philosophers by Paul F. Lazarsfeld; Philosophy of science and empirical social research, in Ernest Nagel, Patrick Suppes and Alfred Tarski, eds.: *Logic, Methodology and Philosophy of Science*, Stanford, Stanford University Press, 1962.

[4]For a survey of many behavioral fields of inquiry see Rollo Handy and Paul Kurtz: *A Current Appraisal of the Behavioral Sciences*, Great Barrington, Mass., Behavioral Research Council, 1964. Also serialized in *The American Behavioral Scientist* in seven Supplements, September 1963 through March 1964.

In view of that situation, the aim here is to concentrate on the controversies that are widely discussed in a variety of behavioral fields. However, from time to time issues that have not yet received wide attention in some fields are included, and some issues are raised that few working scientists in any discipline are overtly concerned about. In short, the purpose is to try to cast some light on general methodological problems by concentrating major attention on those controversies that the scientists involved recognize as significant. It is not assumed that the scientists are correct in their views as to what is most significant for future progress, but a reasonable working principle is to emphasize those issues.

3. TYPE OF LANGUAGE USED

Humanists are fond of criticizing the uncouth and murky jargon used by behavioral scientists. Although the present writer agrees that this criticism is often justifiable, the critics often come with depressingly unclean hands. Literary criticism, philosophic productions, and other humanistic writings often abound in language incomprehensible not only to outsiders but also to other insiders. With high frequency humans tend to obfuscation in those contexts in which they either have nothing to say or do not understand what they are trying to talk about. The sham, pretentiousness, and obscurity so often encountered lead one to suspect that the late development of language behavior in the evolutionary process is responsible for man's inept handling of symbols.

Some insight into this problem as it bears on the present essay may be gained through discussion of an article by James K. Senior, a chemist—an article that does not seem to have provoked much reaction on the part of philosophers.[5] Although his primary concern is with the physical sciences, much of what he says is applicable to behavioral inquiry. Senior argues that the working scientist is ordinarily "bilingual." He has command over the laboratory vernacular that constitutes his customary mode of communication with colleagues. He has much less adequate command over the language used to discuss methodological issues ("metascience"). Senior calls this latter language a kind of scientific *hochdeutsch*. The

[5]James K. Senior: The vernacular of the laboratory, *Philosophy of Science*, 25, 1958.

laboratory vernacular, although highly successful for its purposes, according to Senior, is neither accurate nor definite, for it has little need to be either. Senior goes on to say that very often technical terms are ostensively introduced to the scientist in the course of his education. The lack of emphasis on careful and adequate verbal specification for the terms does not hinder communication, if the people involved have had similar conditioning. But difficulties multiply when people lacking that conditioning attempt to communicate using those terms. Especially confusing is the situation in which the philosopher of science puts emphasis on the *hochdeutsch* language; he frequently will find the scientists naive, incoherent, or even unintelligible. Senior believes that an adequate rapport between the metascience inquirers and the laboratory workers cannot be gained until the methodologists realize that the scientist's command of *hochdeutsch* may be feeble indeed.

Others, too, have discussed the tendency of philosophers to over-emphasize certain linguistic aspects of the full scientific process. Thomas M. Nelson and S. Howard Bartley argue that some confuse empirical science as an activity practiced by humans with a specific type of "artifact" that may result from that activity—the construction of a theoretical language.[6] Instrumentalists have often criticized what they regard as overly formal accounts of scientific inquiry for neglecting the more mundane aspects of science, including pounding, squeezing, etc.[7] In short, the language used by working scientists to describe the methodological aspects of their inquiries is often grossly inadequate (and may tend to oversimplify relatively complex activities); while philosophers of science often neglect the context of scientific inquiry and focus attention only on the final result. As a result, all too often what strikes the philosopher as a highly useful methodological clarification may strike the scientists as irrelevant.

The satisfactory use of the vernacular *within* a field may not yield equally good results when used in other fields or in interdisciplinary

---

[6]Thomas M. Nelson and S. Howard Bartley: Numerosity, number, arithmetization, measurement and psychology, *Philosophy of Science, 28*, 1961.

[7]For a clear succinct statement of this point of view, see George R. Geiger, An experimentalist approach to education, in Nelson B. Henry, ed.: *Modern Philosophies and Education*, Chicago, National Society for the Study of Education, 1955, pt. I, p. 140.

efforts. Just because the verbal specifications of terms are inadequate, those having a different conditioning, education, experience, etc., than the users of those terms may fail to comprehend what is being said. Although similar or identical problems arise in many of the behavioral fields, the differing contexts, terminology, and interests of the inquirers often obscure similarities, and there is little chance to profit by what other workers have thought and said. And frequently philosophers of science have their work judged, not by the relevance it may have for the problems of the working scientist, but by prevailing fashions in philosophy.

Finally, another problem has some bearing on the issue of effective communication. Within the various disciplines of the behavioral sciences very different proportions of effort have been devoted to general methodological questions. For example, although many psychologists are deeply concerned about methodology, well-acquainted with the history of scientific method, and generally sophisticated in their approaches, until recently, at least, sociologists were naive by comparison. And workers in history, jurisprudence, and political science who are interested in conducting their inquiries in a scientific manner sometimes seem crude in their discussions of questions such as "What constitutes scientific method?"

Since communication between scientists in different fields of activity, and communication between scientists and philosophers, is so often poor and ineffective, and since humans in general are so prone to practice verbal magic, a decision was made to avoid as much technical terminology as possible in the present monograph, and also to avoid modes of language that are highly specific to one field.[8] The danger of taking a merely verbal solution for something else is an ever present one, and not only in the behavioral sciences. A remark by K. S. Lashley, made some time ago, is still instructive:

> ". . . it is doubtful that we know anything more about the mechanism of learning than did Descartes when he described the open-

---

[8]Although anyone who has read even the first few pages would not be in danger of thinking that the present author supports "ordinary language" philosophy, the mention of technical language may make it wise to deny specifically such affiliation. The denial by supporters of that movement that its critics understand what they are criticizing, however, makes for some problems.

ing of the pores in the nerves by the passage of animal spirits. His statement sounds remarkably like the reduction of synaptic resistance by the passage of the nerve-impulse."[9]

However, this is not to imply that technical language in general is unnecessary. Such language obviously often leads to more effective, economical, and adequate communication than does folk language. Abuses of technical terminology may abound without in the least militating against the need for such terminology.

Various views can be found in the literature as to how close to common sense behavioral science theories should be. Max Black, for example, has maintained that to the extent that the history of natural sciences is a guide, social theory will have to use "recondite notions, at a considerable remove from direct observation," if an adequate research framework is to be achieved.[10] On the other hand, Lewis Feuer has challenged Black on just this point and maintains both that many notions in physics are not "recondite" and also that we need not assume that social theory requires such notions.[11] Rather than trying to judge *a priori* just how recondite the notions of the behavioral sciences should be, the view here is that whatever notions are necessary to further prediction and control should be employed.

4. WHAT ARE THE BEHAVIORAL SCIENCES?

Many terminological disputes and differences occur relating to this issue. Although certain types of problems seem generally agreed upon as belonging to the *behavioral* or *social* sciences, there is less agreement as to how these terms should be specified. As a first, relatively crude approximation, those problems referred to are the problems of men in society. Many of the inquiries conducted in economics, sociology, psychology, history, political science, anthropology, jurisprudence, information theory, decision theory, communication theory, etc., can thus be classified together. The specific techniques so useful in the physical and physiological sciences do

[9]K. S. Lashley: Nervous mechanisms in learning, in Carl A. Murchison, ed.: *A Handbook of General Experimental Psychology*, Worcester, Mass., Clark University Press, 1934, p. 493.

[10]Max Black: *op. cit.*, p. 279.

[11]In his review of the Black volume on Parsons: *Journal of Philosophy*, LIX:190, 1962.

not seem adequate (at least as yet) for the solution of the problems under discussion.

Although these problems are often labeled "social science" problems, such labeling may lead to the exclusion of much of psychology, on the ground that psychology is concerned with individual, rather than social, matters. Even ignoring other skeptical doubts about such a classification, however, an immediate question arises concerning the field of social psychology. And, at least in the hands of some users, "social science" seems to exclude those biological phenomena that bear directly on so-called social phenomena.

The popularity in recent years of the phrase "behavioral science" indicates that it may be useful. However, some users construe that label broadly enough to include many nonhuman forms of behavior, such as the behavior of atoms, stars, etc. According to James G. Miller, the term "behavioral sciences" was coined about 1949 by a group of University of Chicago scientists who were concerned with the development of a testable general theory of behavior. He says the name was adopted for two reasons: a) its "neutral" flavor would make it acceptable to both social and biological scientists; b) the scientists envisaged the future possibility of asking for financial support from people who might confuse "social science" with "socialism."[12] Whatever we think of the second reason, this use has the merit of not excluding psychology, or parts of it, but it may confuse some significant distinctions between the biological and the social realms of inquiry.

Somewhat reluctantly, but in order to have a brief convenient label, the term "behavioral science" will be adopted in this essay. The intention here is *not* to include all possible forms of behavior, but rather human behavior of certain types. Precise delineation of those types will not be attempted for several reasons. a) As scientific progress continues, it is possible that "purely" physiological inquiries will throw considerable light on social behavior. b) Even in present circumstances, the prediction of human behavior is often facilitated by an awareness of material from other realms of inquiry, as is shown by an example Ernest Nagel gives in his criticism of a view advocated by F. A. Hayek and others. These writers hold that

---

[12] James G. Miller: Toward a general theory for the behavioral sciences, *The American Psychologist, 10:*513, 1955.

human purposive behavior can only be inquired into on the basis of the alleged intentions, beliefs, etc. (subjective states), of the humans involved, and that scientific knowledge that those humans are unaware of is irrelevant to the understanding of their behavior.

For example, it is sometimes said that if a given group of people lacks our present knowledge about the properties of a particular medicine, that knowledge is simply irrelevant to the explanation of the actions of those people. But, as Nagel argues, although pre-Civil War southern cotton planters lacked our contemporary information about soil chemistry and mistakenly thought that the continued use of animal manure would indefinitely maintain soil fertility, a behavioral scientist's awareness of modern chemistry can explain why the cotton soil gradually deteriorated and hence why there was an increasing need for new land.[13] c) In any event it seems pointless and foolish to try to legislate in advance what will or will not prove to be helpful in inquiring into human behavior. Sharp mind-body, subjective-objective, individual-social, etc., distinctions have a way of evaporating in inquiry, and are more useful in establishing neat and tidy pigeonholes for researches than in furthering them.

However, this should not blind us to a kind of unity pervading many of the problems here called behavioral. To a great extent they involve human communication, language use, or what may be called sign-behavior.[14] Without precluding either the present or future use of physical and physiological techniques, it is apparent that at present such techniques are of relatively little help in the description, prediction, and explanation of sign-behavior. Also, it is just this type of behavior that is often held to be unamenable to controlled scientific inquiry because it is "mental," or "subjective," or "nonnatural," or "free." The door is then opened for various substitutes for scientific inquiry, including intuition, *verstehen*, and Wittgensteinian "understanding."

[13]Ernest Nagel: *The Structure of Science*, New York, Harcourt, Brace & World, 1961, pp. 475-76.

[14]"Sign" is here used approximately as John Dewey and Arthur F. Bentley use it in their *Knowing and the Known*, Boston, Beacon Press, 1949. On p. 301 they emphasize that "sign" is to be "understood always as sign-process; never with localization of sign either in organism or in environment separately taken." The philosophic aversion to this volume may be partly due to its opaque passages, but even so it is difficult to understand why the book has not been taken more seriously.

5. ASPECTS OF SCIENTIFIC INQUIRY

It is a commonplace that both historically and in the present, diverse notions of what constitutes scientific inquiry can be found. Many disputes as to whether or not a given inquiry can be pursued scientifically involve not only empirical questions, but competing notions of "scientific." The present author has a general sympathy with those who attempt to develop their notion of "scientific" on the basis of what scientists actually do. But even if this is accepted, problems abound. Some preliminary comments as to why this is so may be helpful.

The internal changes within scientific disciplines are sources of difficulty. A given area of inquiry may undergo rather rapid and far-reaching development in a relatively short time, and then remain static for a long period. A particular discipline may lag far behind what has been achieved in another, similar, discipline. Some of the best work of a given time and place may seem woefully inadequate as judged by the criteria of a later time or different place. But in a sense these changes can be allowed for, and frequently pose no great difficulty if the historical context is kept in mind.

More subtle difficulties stem from differing valuations put upon scientific inquiry in varying social and cultural contexts. For example, in the last decade some of the workers in general systems theory have been as speculative as the absolute idealists were, and yet those same workers may insist that their efforts are scientific. If the social prestige of science were not so great, they might be inclined to call their efforts philosophical.

Various traditions within disciplines, and types of education, may also play a part. Some, conditioned to be hostile toward science, may practice what is here regarded as carefully controlled scientific work while at the same time denying that their inquiries are scientific. Others are so inculcated with the merits and prospects of science that they regard almost everything they do as scientific. Attempts to specify with some degree of adequacy what a given author intends to include and exclude in his use of "scientific inquiry" are often disheartening, if not depressing. The topic is apparently not easily compressed into a short space.

Hence the solution adopted here is to avoid any attempt to give a definitive or final answer, or even a complete answer within specified limits. Rather the emphasis is on discussing some aspects of scientific method that are controversial, with the aim of making clear to readers what is intended by the present author when he discusses scientific inquiry. The views on science advocated here have been much influenced by the writings of John Dewey and J. R. Kantor.[15] The obscurity of much of what Dewey wrote makes it difficult to say with confidence whether my understanding of Dewey is correct. In any event, even assuming a correct understanding of Dewey, there is no intention to agree with him always. Kantor's work has been neglected or thought of minimal value by many philosophers. Partly this may be a result of his style and his terminology. His view of science is in many ways healthy, perceptive, and subtle, although as in the case of Dewey, there are many divergences between his views and those of this monograph.

The conviction of the present author is that the unsatisfactory nature of many accounts of scientific method is largely attributable to the ahistorical and noncontextual view of science often adopted. The hope of saying once and for all what constitutes scientific inquiry is an alluring one for many. The difficulty, of course, is that some activities practically everyone agrees should be labeled "scientific" just do not fall within those descriptions. A great virtue of Dewey and Kantor is their refusal to fall into such a trap.

Not the least of the ironies one encounters is the methodologist of science, who after laying justifiably great emphasis on the fact that the propositions within science are all subject to change, modification, or elimination, then allows the "quest for certainty" to infect him and lays down absolutes in his accounts of scientific methodology.[16] A full list of the idols advocated would be tedious, but to mention a few may be useful. Some writers, not long ago, searched for protocol sentences, and frequently the search proved as fruitless as that for the Kantian noumena. Presently we find those who have discovered that scientists are map-makers, and we have charming if inconsequential talk about different terrains. Others have made

---

[15]In the case of Dewey, the preceding reference and his *Logic: The Theory of Inquiry*, New York, Holt, 1938, have been most influential. In the case of Kantor, his *The Logic of Modern Science*, Bloomington, Ind., Principia Press, 1953, deserves citation.

[16]As sometimes happens with Felix Kaufmann, in his interesting *Methodology of the Social Sciences*, New York, Oxford University Press, 1944.

noncontradiction the greatest deity of all, and a jealous god it has turned out to be.

Probably any brief characterization of science is seriously inadequate. The view presented by R. B. Braithwaite, allowing for its brevity, would be acceptable to many. He holds that the function of a science (with "science" being used in fairly close conformity to "the most frequent modern use of the word") is:

> ". . . to establish general laws covering the behaviour of the empirical events or objects with which the science in question is concerned, and thereby to enable us to connect together our knowledge of the separately known events, and to make reliable predictions of events as yet unknown. . . . The fundamental concept for science is thus that of scientific law, and the fundamental aim of a science is the establishment of such laws."[17]

To facilitate understanding of the views of the present author, Braithwaite's comments will be taken as the point of departure, and deviation of the views presented in this monograph from the prevailing ones will become clear. Let us begin first with the notions of *prediction* and *control*. These are sometimes taken as basic to the scientific enterprise. Perhaps at this juncture no great problems arise with *prediction*, but some have challenged its linkage with *control*. Those advocating the importance of control have sometimes left themselves open to the charge of ignoring the fact that impressive predictions are possible in situations in which control is not humanly possible; e.g., the prediction of eclipses. However, if the notion of adjustive behavior appropriate to situations in which control is not possible is added, we shall do justice to the usual intentions of those emphasizing control. Many situations occur in which no human control is (at least now) possible, but accurate predictions enable us to behave in a way appropriate to the situation.

Yet we should be fully aware that the type and degree of prediction and control vary historically. In a given time and place a great accomplishment might consist in a rough prediction that at another time and place would seem so crude as to hardly deserve the label "scientific." If in a given situation no human control was heretofore possible, the rudimentary beginnings of control may similarly be a

---

[17]Richard B. Braithwaite: *Scientific Explanation*, New York, Harper, 1960, pp. 1-2.

great gain, as in the control of a disease. Yet as medicine develops, much higher standards of control may be insisted upon. It seems pointless to ask for some definitely specifiable degree of either prediction or control in advance; a contextual approach makes more sense and frees us from unwelcome rigidities. For example, some recent work in social psychology on "experimenter bias" in areas concerning supposedly objective experimental findings indicates that the experimenters "are able to obtain from their human or animal" subjects the data that the experimenters "want, need, or expect to get."[18]

This is not to say that so-called *postdiction* or *retrodiction* is unimportant or insignificant. But typically major scientific interest in such phenomena develops in the hope of aiding prediction and control. Nor is it to deny that many technical problems, logical and methodological, arise in connection with prediction and postdiction. Yet the view maintained here is that *in the context* of the scientist's work on a given problem, the technical questions which so preoccupy philosophers often have relatively little significance. What counts as a "reliable prediction," then, is historically and technologically relative and may be comfortably accepted as such. From the point of view of the inquirer, some of the technical questions of confirmation, the basis of induction, etc., have minor importance, no matter how dear they are to philosophers. The *only* objection to the detailed treatment of such questions raised here concerns cases in which philosophers insist that such questions are either prior to the resolution of scientific inquiry or of great import for the success of that inquiry. In their own way, in other contexts, and for other purposes, those questions may be significant, interesting, and deserving of great attention.

This, then, leads us to an issue that can be put in many ways and discussed from many angles. If I read the current literature correctly, it is widely regarded as old hat, if not superficial, to say that the ultimate aim is to control nature for man's benefit. This is said to reek of an "outmoded" confidence in human progress, to be

---

[18]R. Rosenthal, K. L. Fode, C. J. Friedman and L. L. Vikan: Subjects' perception of their experimenter under conditions of experimenter bias, *Perceptual and Motor Skills, 11:*325, 1960. See also, R. Rosenthal and K. L. Fode: The effect of experimenter bias on the performance of the albino rat, *Behavioral Science, 8*, 1963.

a throwback to the Enlightenment, or excessively optimistic. To be sure, sometimes confident statements about the aims of science are expressed more rhetorically than critically and open the door to many objections. On the other hand, it is difficult to see what is so terrible about regarding science as receiving its historical impetus from its ability to modify nature (including man). It may not be fashionable, but if one adopts the view that scientific inquiry is a human institution with definite sociocultural roots, it becomes plausible to explain the rise of science partially in terms of the new control of nature possible through it.

One may retain, then, the Enlightenment view that the social function of science is to further our control over nature (including adjustive behavior thereto), and still discuss the intellectual function of science as the establishment of "general laws." However, "law" is used in so many ways that one may be pardoned for having some suspicion of that term. There seems to be at least some tendency these days to proceed along the lines that Braithwaite adopts, and use "general law" to include not only some of the much publicized general laws of physics, but also generalizations of the "natural history" sort, such as "all whales are mammals."[19] Others, of course, do not make "law" so inclusive. In order to encompass both the so-called "highly developed" and the "lesser developed" sciences, the phrase used here will be Dewey's "warranted assertion." In passing, it may be observed that some uses of "higher" development are assumptive in the extreme. Does "higher" mean from the point of view of the methodological formalist, or from the point of view of the type of successful predictions achieved, or something else?

"Warranted assertion" has several virtues. It apparently helps to exorcise the lingering ghost that science has uncovered (or will uncover) final, fixed, and incorrigible generalizations, or "ideals," or other closures to inquiry. It also helps to concentrate attention on the fact that the assertion in question is warranted by a definite process of inquiry, presumably open to replication and subject to other tests. This also relates to the previous discussion, in which it was maintained that there is both historical and technological relativity as to what is regarded as well-established in a given scientific

---

[19]Braithwaite: *op. cit.*, pp. 1-2.

discipline. Further, one is freed from the only too attractive "problem" of arranging sciences in some type of hierarchy based on the kind of alleged law those sciences have ascertained. A warranted assertion with its ground, justification, or warrant open to inspection and criticism, and with the range of application specified, seems to be the immediate end product of scientific inquiries.

As has become evident, considerable emphasis in this essay is placed on the notion that all scientific assertions are to be regarded as subject to modification, correction, and elimination. This is what Felix Kaufmann, in his discussion of procedural rules, calls "the principle of permanent control."[20] Although even some eminent working scientists have thought they had firmly in hand an absolute not subject to that principle, historically the development of an insistence that there are no assertions so privileged has been an enormous spur to the success of scientific inquiry. Although it has taken some revolutions in physical science to make the lesson clear, increasingly the principle of permanent control is given an important place, at least on the "official" level.

In the case of some behavioral scientists, however, the principle is denied, and the ascertainment of certain incorrigible truths is undertaken with considerable confidence. To cite but one example, Ludwig von Mises asserts that economics has a unique position because "its particular theorems are not open to any verification or falsification on the ground of experience. . . . The ultimate yardstick of an economic theorem's correctness or incorrectness is solely reason unaided by experience."[21] Such views, maintained boldly and frankly, may be respected on just those grounds. More difficult to handle are those who insist on the corrigibility of all scientific assertions, but at the same time search for, and occasionally "find," some incorrigible fundamentals.[22]

---

[20]Kaufmann: *op. cit.*, p. 39 and Ch. IV.

[21]Ludwig von Mises: *Human Action: A Treatise on Economics*, New Haven, Yale University Press, 1949, p. 858.

[22]A penetrating criticism of what he labels "fundamentalism" in the theory of measurement is given by C. West Churchman in his essay, A materialist theory of measurement, in R. W. Sellars, V. J. McGill, and Marvin Farber, eds.: *Philosophy for the Future*, New York, Macmillan, 1949. Mario Bunge has also criticized fundamentalism in his *The Myth of Simplicity*, Englewood Cliffs, N. J., Prentice-Hall, 1963, Ch. 6, and in his *Intuition and Science*, Englewood Cliffs, N. J., Prentice-Hall, 1962, Ch. 1.

The principle of permanent control helps to make sense of the *objectivity* that characterizes the results of successful scientific inquiry. Those who admit that at least some scientific disciplines have achieved a high degree of objectivity are sometimes prone to give this a mentalistic or moralistic interpretation. Scientists, unlike other men, are said to be objective, or so honest that impartiality and fidelity to the "facts" necessarily characterize their efforts. A more helpful explanation of the objectivity often achieved is based on the way scientific inquiry has become institutionalized. One need not attribute special traits to scientists to account for the honesty, rigor, and impartiality of their results. Fortunately, at least in physical science disciplines, the penalties for falsification of data, nonduplicable experiments, etc., are so great that only rarely are certain canons of research violated.

Of course the picture is not uniformly rosy. Special intellectual interests may inhibit the publication of results displeasing to those interests; novel conclusions, no matter how well based, may be ignored for long periods; and academic politics may play a conspicuous role at times. Kantor mentions some interesting cases, including the refusal of the *Royal Society Transactions* to publish Benjamin Franklin's electrical experiments.[23] An intriguing case, as reported by Robert Jungk, concerns Madame Irene Joliot-Curie's famous experiments in the 1930's. The acceptance of new experimental findings was hindered by a variety of circumstances, including the rivalry between Madame Joliot-Curie and Fraulein Lise Meitner, the political tensions and rivalries between France and Germany at that time, and the threat to accepted nuclear theory. At a conference in 1933 Madame Joliot and her husband presented the results derived from the bombardment of aluminum with neutrons. Fraulein Meitner got different results, and apparently most of the physicists at the conference agreed that the Joliots' experiments were inaccurate. The next major achievement of the Joliots concerned artificial radioactivity, and again their results were thought to be unreliable. At least one prominent German scientist initially refused even to read the paper summarizing the achievement. Finally, in Germany Otto Hahn and F. Strassmann

[23]Kantor: *op. cit.*, p. 57. His entire Ch. 3, Scientific enterprises as cultural institutions, is well worth reading.

did verify that the bombardment of uranium with neutrons produced a new substance, which they found to be barium. But the threat to accepted views was so great that Hahn and Strassmann felt it necessary to say that although as chemists they had to affirm that barium, not radium, was the result, as nuclear scientists they could not take a step so at odds with all previous findings in nuclear physics.[24] In short, it would be excessively naive to assume that extrascientific factors do not sometimes have a significant influence on the acceptance of new views, and it is always dangerous to underestimate the influence of accepted beliefs.

One also is entitled to have a certain skepticism about the influence of so-called traditional "values" or "ideal" types of behavior of scientists. A study reported by S. S. West attempted to assess the correlation between the rate of publication and the "strength of motivation toward research as judged by peers," on the one hand, and the assumed traditional values on the other. The latter values were "freedom in research, impartiality, suspension of judgment until sufficient evidence is at hand, absence of bias, diffusion of information, and group loyalty." A total of 57 science faculty members of a midwestern university were studied (7 anatomists, 9 biochemists, 17 mathematicians, 9 physicists, 7 physiologists, and 8 sociologists). Various controls were instituted, and the conclusion arrived at was:

> "One may infer, then, that neither rate of publication nor strength of motivation toward research (as judged by peers) is more than quite weakly related to adherence to the classical ideology of science."

> "It is concluded that the classical morality of science is not associated to any important degree with productive research."[25]

---

[24]Robert Jungk: *Brighter than a Thousand Suns: A Personal History of the Atomic Scientists*, James Cleugh, tr., New York, Harcourt, Brace, 1958, pp. 62-68. Mention may also be made of a recent issue of *The American Behavioral Scientist*, *VII*: 1, 1963, devoted to the Velikovsky case. Even if the contributors to that issue are mistaken in a great number of instances, the evidence of the bearing nonscientific factors may have on the evaluation of scientific materials is impressive.

[25]S. S. West: The ideology of academic scientists, *IRE Transactions of the Professional Group on Engineering Management*, 1960, Vol. EM-7, pp. 54, 61. In view of the sample size, no assertion is made here that West's results are applicable to all or most scientists, but rather it is held that his results are an interesting straw in the wind.

Doubtless a multitude of examples could be cited, but the strife in the physical and physiological sectors of science appears mild compared to that in the behavioral sectors. The reasons seem clear enough. The insistence in the "hard science" areas on empirical verification of a kind relatively unaffected by social, cultural, and economic contexts assures the elimination of much that is unsound and the relatively rapid acceptance and promulgation of that which is sound. As yet similar "ground rules" are not institutionalized for behavioral areas. Hence prestige often is heavily awarded to ingenious theories, new approaches, alleged breakthroughs, etc. And, of course, even in areas in which there is a body of widely accepted data, different interpretations may occur. If significant enough human consequences are involved, even in the hard science areas there can be emotional strife. Recent controversies among scientists as to the danger of fallout are a case in point. The best approach seems to be the development in the behavioral areas of "rules of the game" parallel to those in the physical sciences. How to achieve this is a complex matter, but such effort seems more intelligent than hoping that a certain type of training or "mental discipline" will insure the desired objectivity on the part of the behavioral scientists. To conclude this section, then, what is here understood by "scientific inquiry" is the prediction and control (and/or adjustive behavior thereto) of events through the development of publicly verifiable warranted assertions that are subject to continuous criticism. The allocation of social resources for scientific inquiry rests largely on the successes that inquiry has achieved and its promise for the future modification of events.

To forestall certain criticisms, it may be helpful to say explicitly that the present author fully recognizes both that prevailing views of scientific inquiry are less "pragmatic" than the one presented here and that many eminent scientists, past and present, would deviate markedly from the views advocated here. There is no intention at all to deny that some scientists want to develop explanations of phenomena that will subjectively satisfy them, that others want to develop a highly formal axiomatic approach, and that still others have no concern for the possible uses of their findings in the solution of human problems. What is maintained is that the present view, tentatively held, is helpful in understanding the sociocultural role of scientific inquiry, and offers a framework for grasping the import of what is done in scientific research. Putting the matter another way, people called scientists behave in certain ways in their professional capacities. They may or may not offer satisfactory descriptions of the methodology underlying their inquiries. And some patterns of behavior of those called scientists may be inconsistent with other patterns. However inadequately, the view advocated here attempts to assess the main lines of scientific inquiry, but no attempt is made to encompass everything that has been done under the label "science."

2

THE THEORETICIAN AND THE LABORATORIAN

1. THE PROBLEM

IN treatises written by both philosophers and behavioral scientists, one finds accounts of the "proper" relation between theory and the collection of data. The contrast between the two aspects of scientific inquiry will be marked in this essay by the use of "theoretician" to refer to the maker of hypotheses or systems of hypotheses, and "laboratorian" to the maker, not only of controlled experiments, but also to the collector of data through field work, naturalistic observation, etc.

In many instances, behavioral scientists give essentially the same account of the relation between the theoretician and the laboratorian as do many philosophic texts. Two such examples may be cited from behavioral disciplines in which controversy occurs on the issue. The editors of a volume advocating a scientific (behavioralist) approach in political science say of their view:

"It stresses the mutual interdependence of theory and research. Theoretical questions need to be stated in operational terms for purposes of empirical research. And, in turn, empirical findings should have a bearing on the development of political theory."[1]

Bert F. Hoselitz argues that:

"Economists today tend to proceed in their research by a common method, which is in its chief aspects identical with the procedures of any empirical science, i.e., the testing of theories by relating them to empirically observable data."[2]

---

[1] Heinz Eulau, Samuel J. Eldersveld and Morris Janowitz, eds.: *Political Behavior: A Reader in Theory and Research*, Glencoe, Ill., Free Press, 1956, p. 4.

[2] Bert F. Hoselitz: Economics, in Bert F. Hoselitz, ed.: *A Reader's Guide to the Social Sciences*, Glencoe, Ill., Free Press, 1959, p. 139.

On the other hand, some workers in a wide variety of behavioral disciplines either explicitly maintain that certain assertions are not subject to empirical test, or show remarkably little interest in that testing. And some workers either explicitly say they do not make use of hypotheses or theories, or tend to emphasize strongly the so-called "pure" gathering of data. In many areas, major discussions turn on the range of theories; in sociology for example, much has been written on the importance of middle-range theories. Sometimes "theory" is used in a way rather different from that most philosophers are accustomed to; certain dimensions of the general problem having considerable interest for many behavioral scientists are only infrequently, if at all, discussed by philosophers. An indication of this can be gained from a comment by Alvin G. Goldstein, which will be discussed later:

> "In psychology, most theories are stated before enough solid information has been collected, and as a result there is a ridiculous profusion of 'theories.' This kind of eagerness is sometime (sic) defended on the basis that a theory will assist the investigator in his search for a solution. Undoubtedly it will if it is accurate, but just as surely will it hinder his quest if it is erroneous. I do not want to get embroiled in the argument about the impossibility of collecting any data without a 'theory'—which again is a misuse of the word—but there is a lot to say for an attitude which can be expressed as 'Let's find out as much as we can about this phenomenon.' "[3]

2. EXTREME THEORETICAL EMPHASES

For convenience, we may group together approaches that either are highly formalistic, or insist that some statements are not subject to empirical falsification, or that emphasize the value of elaborating a complex theoretical structure in the absence of empirical testing. Examples will be given from economics, sociology, psychology, and game theory.

Leland B. Yeager has argued that although it is impossible to check economic theorems in the "real" world, they can be checked in a direct way "not available to natural scientists":

---

[3] Alvin G. Goldstein, review of *Development of the Perceptual World*, by C. M. Solley and G. Murphy: *Philosophy of Science, 29:*326, 1962.

"It is understandable that to people trained in the natural sciences, the method of economic theory may smack of Kantianism and its synthetic *a priori* . . . Anthropomorphism, rightly scorned in the natural sciences as pre-scientific metaphysics, is justified in economics because economics is about human action. . ."[4]

In sociology so many disputes have centered on the work of Talcott Parsons that attention may profitably be given to those controversies. There is considerable disagreement as to just what status Parsons' theory has. A. W. Gouldner has argued that Parsons' theory of the social system tends to direct research efforts away from systematic attempts "to develop and validate generalized propositions concerning the manner in which ecological and other properties of the physical environment of groups structure patterns of social organization." Excluding such properties from the social system, he goes on, gives Parsons only a purely formal advantage. While it may help to make social science autonomous, it also "may be a Pyrrhic victory bought at the cost of a scientific ritualism, where logical elegance is substituted for empirical potency."[5] This would seem to treat Parsons' theory as an attempt to develop hypotheses that explain social behavior.

Others, however, have maintained that Parsons' theory is not an attempt to develop such hypotheses, but is rather, to use Parsons' own words, "a logically articulated conceptual scheme." Thus Henry Landsberger says that in Parsons' theory the sectors and subsectors are primarily "pigeonholes for the ordering of problems."[6] Max Black regards many of Parsons' principles not as empirical generalizations of great scope but as analytic consequences of the notion of "human action."[7] Lewis Feuer argues that even so, "great advances in social science" have occurred precisely through the exploration of what, from a certain standpoint, are analytic con-

---

[4]Leland B. Yeager: Measurement as scientific method in economics, *American Journal of Economics and Sociology*, *16*:344, 1957.

[5]A. W. Gouldner: Reciprocity and autonomy in functional theory, in Llewellyn Gross, ed.: *Symposium on Sociological Theory*, Evanston, Row, Peterson, & Co., 1959, p. 246.

[6]Henry Landsberger: Parsons' theory of organizations, in Max Black, ed.: *The Social Theories of Talcott Parsons: A Critical Examination*, Englewood Cliffs, N. J., Prentice-Hall, 1961, p. 233.

[7]In Max Black: *op. cit.*, pp. 282-83.

sequences of definitions; but at the same time he has little confidence that such advances will occur under the stimulus of Parsonian theory.[8]

Thus various interpretations have been given of what Parsons' theory is best viewed as, and it would hardly be surprising if more interpretations were to appear in the future. The major questions seem to be the extent to which links can be supplied between his theory (however construed) and observable behavior; and if such linkage can be supplied, the extent to which his theory helps to predict and control that behavior.

In psychology, learning theories often have had a highly deductive character, and Clark L. Hull's hypothetical-deductive approach to behaviorism has attracted much attention. To some critics it has had the fatal defect of not being amenable to testing. Sigmund Koch, for example, argues that Hull's theory has gaps, inconsistencies, and indeterminacies that make it untestable.[9]

To cite but one more instance, some of the strongest criticism of various developments in such new areas as game theory is that basic assumptions are made in order to develop deductive consequences but that little or no attention is given to the extent to which those assumptions are in accord with observed behavior. Certainly some of the advocates of those newer approaches are quite convinced that their assumptions are either so self-evident or intuitive that they hardly need testing. Robert H. Strotz, for example, although aware that empirical testing is desirable, says some of the axioms of game theory have "strong intuitive appeal," and that every "normal person would clearly accept them as precepts of behavior."[10]

In short, the hope of many writers inclining in this direction seems to be a naive version (naive in view of some of the well-established results of anthropology and psychology) of the hope animating some of the classical philosophical rationalists. If one can begin with certainty and then deduce valid consequences, the consequences will be as certain as the axioms. Stated so baldly, it may seem inconceivable that anyone would so argue about be-

[8]Lewis Feuer, review of Max Black: *op. cit.*, *Journal of Philosophy*, LIX:188 ff., 1962.
[9]Sigmund Koch: Clark L. Hull, in William K. Estes, ed.: *Modern Learning Theory: A Critical Analysis of Five Examples*, New York, Appleton-Century-Crofts, 1954.
[10]Robert H. Strotz: Cardinal utility, *American Economic Review*, XLIII:391-93, 1953.

havioral science materials. And, to be sure, defenses of the highly formal, deductive approaches are usually couched much more circumspectly, if not deviously. Yet sometimes such a view is clearly and straightforwardly advocated. Thus the sociologist, Arnold Rose, suggests that sociologists may learn much from the deductive approaches of such economists as Adam Smith, the Utilitarians, Jevons, and Marshall. Beginning with truisms, tautologies, or so-called self-evident truths, predictions would be deduced, and then sociologists might develop "interconnected logical propositions from which important deductions and predictions could be derived that have as much validity as their original assumptions."[11] Rose further seems to think that those original assumptions could have great "validity."

3. EXTREME LABORATORIAN EMPHASES

So-called "brute," or "rudimentary," or "merely descriptive" empiricism is under severe attack these days. Frequently one finds expressions of relief that such and such fields of inquiry are at last free from an overly simplistic empiricism. The usual criticisms of such an approach are that elimination of explicit theory may result in bias stemming from an implicit theory; that the results of such empiricism are unrelated to, or unsystematized with, other aspects of science; that a mere collection of alleged facts is not science; etc.[12] Although few behavioral scientists these days want to eschew theory entirely, there is the apparent exception of B. F. Skinner. One of his papers, in which he is unusually critical of philosophers of science, ought to be required reading.[13] He not only neatly punctures much pretentious verbalizing on the part of both phil-osophers and scientists; he helps to focus attention on the actual process of inquiry rather than on the neat final product, the pub-lished paper. On the other hand, although Skinner insists that he "never attacked a problem by constructing a Hypothesis," he re-

[11]Arnold Rose: *Theory and Method in the Social Sciences*, Minneapolis, University of Minnesota Press, 1954, p. 342.

[12]For example, see the remarks by Robert Bierstedt: A critique of empiricism in sociology, *American Sociological Review*, *14*, 1949.

[13]B. F. Skinner: A case history in scientific method, *The American Psychologist*, *11*: 227 and 231, 1956.

veals that he is always searching for "order." In addition, his examples and his argument make clear enough that he is not objecting to what are commonly referred to as hypotheses, but rather to certain types of theories.

Those who emphasize the accurate compilation of data without trying to fit that data into some larger theoretical scheme are of special interest in this context. Perhaps the outstanding example of such an approach is found in the field work of cultural anthropologists. According to C. W. M. Hart, in the main the "sheer description of a natural phenomenon, or of human behavior treated as a natural phenomenon," is still regarded as both a primary duty and a problem in itself.[14] To a considerable extent field work is the major criterion within the profession for judging the work of cultural anthropologists, not the theoretical views that might be developed on the basis of that work.

4. SUMMARY OF CONTEMPORARY VIEWS

A few behavioral inquirers deny the relevance of empirical testing for some of their axioms, basic assumptions, or initial starting points. A few inquirers come close to denying the usefulness of theory. The vast majority, however, do advocate the testing of hypotheses. The controversies concern the extent to which it is possible to test certain hypotheses. The critics of some writers maintain that the theories of those writers are so far ahead of available data that they become almost pointless, or that the theories ignore such empirical data as are already available, or that the theories are so stated as to be not amenable to testing. These views will be discussed, but first several other topics bearing on the issue will be considered: the role of mathematics, the role of models, and theories of the middle-range.

5. THE ROLE OF MATHEMATICS

Several complicating factors are present, if one attempts to survey all the areas here labeled behavioral. The differing traditions of the several areas result in some researchers having had a great deal of

---

[14]C. W. M. Hart: Cultural anthropology and sociology, in Howard Becker and Alvin Boskoff, eds.: *Modern Sociological Theory*, New York, Dryden, 1957, p. 538.

formal education in mathematics, while others have had very little. This helps to account for the fact that some defenses of highly mathematical approaches rely heavily on the notion that if the critics only knew more mathematics, they would see the relevance of what they are criticizing. And to be sure, some objections to mathematicizing are peculiar indeed. Fairly frequently one finds writers who maintain that human behavior is not subject to quantification, and yet those same writers make use of crude quantifying terms much as "more" or "less." What might better be expressed as an objection to more precise quantification than the materials warrant is sometimes expressed as an objection to all quantification.

Even if it is fully agreed that, properly used, mathematics can be of signal aid to inquiry, and even if no semi-mystical or obscurantist objections are entered against the possible use of mathematics, one is entitled to considerable skepticism about many of the attempted applications of mathematics today. The precision, formal elegance and rigor possible in mathematics may tend to blind some workers to what they actually are doing. Although the error is a simple one, there seems to be an always present danger of confusing mathematical transformations, which may follow the highest standards of carefulness, rigor, and adequacy, with verification of what is initially assumed.

Dubious assumptions stated in conventional language do not become either more adequate or less subject to criticism merely because they are translated into mathematical language. The formalization of those assumptions so that mathematical transformations can be performed easily does nothing to show that the assumptions are useful in inquiry. Lest this seem too innocent or too obvious, it will be helpful to consider some recent articles on the methodology of physics. Henry Margenau and Richard A. Mould found it necessary to distinguish sharply between the formal mathematical structure of a physical theory and the "rules of correspondence" that relate the mathematical structure to "immediate experience."[15] In a later paper, Herbert Dingle remarks that such a distinction is

---

[15]Henry Margenau and Richard A. Mould: Relativity: an epistemological appraisal, *Philosophy of Science, 24*:299, 1957.

obviously not new and yet physicists often fail to keep it in mind, with the result that "proof of mathematical consistency is frequently mistaken for evidence of facts of immediate experience, without examination of the validity of the rules of correspondence."[16] Perhaps it is safe to add that if the mathematical work involved requires great ingenuity, skill, and learning, it may be all the more tempting to act as if formal consistency made detailed empirical testing unnecessary or unimportant.

At least on occasion, behavioral inquirers seem especially prone to this sort of thing. As will be discussed later, some developments in economic theory, game theory, decision theory, information theory, etc., call for considerable mathematical ingenuity; so much so that critics untrained to the proper level are left either speechless or fearful of displaying their ignorance by objecting. But it is not difficult to find frequent charges that some of the most admired mathematical structures have little significance from the point of view of testing. To cite but one such example, Richard C. Bernhard says:

"In the social sciences, many models are mathematical formulations using type equations without specific numerical content. The most eminent of these is the Walrasian pure theory of economics, a logical structure of marvelous intricacy and great beauty, but by itself not based on measurements nor leading to experimental verification of deductions from its postulates."[17]

Perhaps only rarely, but still sometimes, one finds a defense of mathematical elaboration independent of any link to observation. Thus Anatol Rapoport has maintained that sometimes observation may contribute almost nothing to the understanding of phenomena, and holds that mathematical physics "would have never left the ground" without "ideally true and factually false laws," such as Galileo's law of falling bodies.[18] The notion of "ideally true" laws

[16]Herbert Dingle: Relativity and electromagnetism: an epistemological appraisal, *Philosophy of Science*, 27:233-34, 1960.

[17]Richard C. Bernhard: Mathematics, models, and language in the social sciences, *Symposia Studies Series No. 3*, The National Institute of Social and Behavioral Science, George Washington University, 1960, p. 2.

[18]Anatol Rapoport: Various meanings of theory, *American Political Science Review*, LII:983, 1958.

can be a slippery one, but presumably it would be peculiar to honor a "law" just because it led to inaccurate predictions. Approximations may be most helpful in prediction, even if "factually false," and yet the observational side of the matter (that in practice good predictions are possible) seems to have the usual importance. The fame of such "laws" would seem to be largely dependent on their utility in predicting observed events, for if they lacked such power there would be little point in calling them "laws."

In summary, although the facility offered by mathematical formulations may be exceptionally helpful, and the precision possible may mark gigantic strides ahead, the mere elaboration of complex mathematical structures that do not aid in prediction, and (more dangerously) the belief that because internal consistency is achieved, insight into human behavior must follow, are to be deplored.

6. THE ROLE OF MODELS

"Model" is a word whose time has come. We find great activity in the construction of models, learned articles on the nature and role of models in science, and even model-centered sciences. At least a trace of skepticism may be in order, for suspicion of verbal magic is generated by the general celebration of modeling. An article by the psychologist, Alphonse Chapanis, offers some enlightenment. He believes that models in psychology are flourishing to a greater extent than ever in the past, and lists various important ways in which models are helpful. Yet his negative comments deserve emphasis. He points out that with high frequency a new model is given great acclaim, but after testing loses its "original aura and enchantment." Specifically mentioned are the servo-model and the model of man as an information-handling system. He also holds that there is something almost magical about the word "model," and that it is customary to call by that label things which a decade ago would have been called "hypothesis," "theory," "hunch," etc. He asserts, after stressing that very often no attention is given to the validation of models, that:

"Even when we find model builders attempting to make some validation of their models we sometimes find them using as scientific evidence the crudest form of observations collected under completely uncontrolled conditions."[19]

In certain respects then, models and mathematically formulated theories may share the same defect: much greater ingenuity, work, skill, and effort goes into the elaboration of the model than into its alleged use in inquiry. Chapanis puts considerable emphasis on the notion that sometimes elaborate models are developed because they are fun for the developer. He contends that the model (containing wires, lights, switches, chemicals, etc.) Clark L. Hull used to illustrate the Presidential address in which he first propounded his formal behavior theory did not explain anything, gave no new insights into conditioned responses, and resulted in no hunches for testing. Chapanis concludes that it was done for the fun of it.

He also gives a fairly detailed discussion of some of the helpful uses of models and some of the dangers in their use. From these lists only one point will be discussed here, since it seems to have some important consequences. Chapanis says that models may encourage the committing of a logical fallacy, that of affirming the consequent. If the model begins with some constants, variables, and assumed relationships, and then deductions are made, it is pleasing indeed to find that those consequences can be verified, and tempting to conclude that the constants, variables, and assumed relations are therefore warranted. As Chapanis also points out, once attention is directed to the formal structure of such an argument, the fallacy is obvious. But when it "appears in the highly disguised form of a mathematical model," we are more easily deceived. In the entire context of inquiry, with the many concerns involved, including possible prestige factors, the desire to get results, and technological problems that may be difficult indeed to solve, it is psychologically easy to affirm the consequent and conclude that the model is indeed a forward step.

Some of the reasons doubt has been expressed about certain applications of models can be understood from a consideration of remarks made by Olaf Helmer and Nicholas Rescher.[20] They refer

---

[19]Alphonse Chapanis: Men, machines, and models, *The American Psychologist, 16:* 130, 1961.

[20]Olaf Helmer and Nicholas Rescher: On the epistemology of the inexact sciences, Santa Monica, California, The RAND Corporation, 1958, (P-1513). The quotations are from pp. 52-54.

to the construction of either mathematical or physical models in which a simulated mathematical or physical object corresponds to "each element of the real situation" and the "relevant properties and relations to other elements are mirrored" by simulated properties and relations. If this has been done properly, one can formulate hypotheses and predictions from the model rather than from "the real world." They conclude that to the extent that the model does accurately simulate "the real world" the results obtained from the model can be translated into corresponding statements about reality. Among the advantages are said to be the possibility of scientific inquiry in situations in which it is too expensive, or physically impossible, or morally impossible, to experiment on "the real-world situation." We may say "so far so good," although it should not be forgotten that problems may arise in the simulation of a model that are as formidable as those arising from direct inquiry into the problematic situation. Unfortunately scale models sometimes do not behave in the way that full size objects do, and the determination of what is relevant may prove difficult. But even so, there are often obvious advantages in the construction of models.

What stimulates considerable doubt is the transition Helmer and Rescher make to inquiries into the behavior of human organizations. They say:

> ". . . the latter can be simulated most effectively by having the experts play the roles of certain members of such organizations and act out what in their judgment would be the actions, in the situation simulated, of their real-life counterparts."

But such short cuts are fraught with annoying problems. If the experts are keenly aware of how organization members would behave in a given situation, role-playing might well be pointless. And surely we have moved a considerable distance from the models our authors mention as being of great use in the applied physical sciences. The objections are not to the use of models *per se*, but rather to the adequacy of the models that sometimes are defended with great optimism. This is not to deny that even a crude form of role-playing may be helpful, but again rather to emphasize how little attention is sometimes given to testing whatever is arrived at through the use of the model.

The general point seems to be clear enough: the principle of permanent control is especially important, in the context of model building as in other contexts. The delights of the model itself do not substitute for verification, and crude verification does not substitute for continued critical testing. This of course is not to say that only thoroughly testable models should be constructed, but rather to point out that often little emphasis is put on the testing. In much of modeling lurks the hope that a relatively simple master model may be uncovered that will answer major questions of human behavior. Until or unless the workers involved habitually emphasize the role of testing, we can expect much theory but little in the way of warranted assertions.

7. THEORIES OF THE MIDDLE-RANGE

As mentioned earlier, in recent years advocacy of middle-range theories has been prominent in sociology.[21] Sometimes it seems to critics that "middle-range" is lamentably vague, or even that it is a device for avoiding difficult theoretical issues. However, if the context is kept in mind, at least some of the vagueness disappears and the point of the advocacy is made clear. From time to time in many of the disciplines there is a great flurry of activity consisting in putting together statistics of relatively little significance. Although such activity may have a point in that it is socially safe, offends no one, is helpful in getting at least small research grants, etc., it often seems to have almost no value for understanding human behavior. In short, the hypotheses employed are so obvious, or so little connected with other hypotheses, warranted assertions, etc., that they are no more than busy-work. However, we should remember that sometimes the obvious is precisely what needs doubting, and what may seem pointless sometimes turns out to have considerable significance.

If at the same time, other highly theoretical constructions are made that for technical or logical reasons are untestable, it becomes clear why middle-range theories are advocated. In other words, "middle-range" is best viewed contextually. What in a formal sense

---

[21]See, for example, the comments by Robert K. Merton: *Social Theory and Social Structure*, Glencoe, Ill., Free Press, 1949, especially p. 97.

seems to be two hypotheses of the same range may seem different if they occur in disciplines of different stages of development. Middle-range theories occupy an intermediate ground between what, in a specific context, appears trivial and what is not subject to test; presumably the greatest chance for successful inquiry would stem from such intermediate theories.

There is considerable difference between defending middle-range theories as being most likely to be fruitful in a given time and place, and defending them as the only proper theories. Although on occasion those noted for their advocacy of these theories may slip from first defense to the second, more likely the critics make the unwarranted transition. In short, some gain may be made by not focusing attention on the *middleness* involved, but rather on the insistence that theoretical and laboratory work be closely related. (This does not take account of the other aspect of the problem, the avoidance of triviality. That issue will be discussed later, in Chapter IV.)

8. ANALYSIS OF THE ISSUES

What are some of the possible merits of the anti-theoretical writers? Their hostility to pretentious, pompous, and sometimes dogmatic theorizing is salutary. Their insistence on confirmation is to be applauded. Their recognition of the hard work necessary to subject a hypothesis to the necessary tests before giving a tentative verdict of "warranted" is to be encouraged. It is fairly clear that many of the anti-theoreticians would admit that they do use hypotheses in the sense of that term normally used by philosophers of science and by a great many working scientists. What they object to is the overly grand use, often capitalized, of "Hypothesis" and "Theory." There also is hostility on their part to the notion that the scientist investigates one precisely stated, abstracted from all else, hypothesis. What often happens, of course, is that the initial hunch is repeatedly reformulated in the context of ongoing inquiry. The most elementary logical framework that might be developed to show what has happened in inquiry can be quite misleading.

Here again the article by Skinner referred to in Section 3 may be mentioned. He shows with great skill some of the changes occurring in inquiry. Indeed, for a brief article, his may be one of the best in describing how a skilled and intelligent inquirer actually works. But it also seems quite evident that Skinner was not just searching for order in the abstract. What he would recognize as order may be influenced by Skinner's awareness of other work, his intelligent guesses as to what might be involved, his insistence on observable events, etc. Oddly enough, although Skinner in no uncertain terms says that he does not function as Dewey thought scientists function, his paper seems to exemplify many of the points advocated in Dewey's *Logic: The Theory of Inquiry.* In summary we can say that in those instances in which generally recognized, worthwhile scientific conclusions have been reached, hypotheses were used, and that what the anti-theoretical but successful scientists are doing is to protest certain theoretical developments rather than the total use of theory.

At this point some attention should be given to a point made by Murray Sidman.[22] Although he recognizes the importance of hypothesis testing, he argues that not all useful experimentation need derive from such testing. He suggests that curiosity may lead an investigator to say "I wonder what would happen if . . ." and those without a firm hypothesis, or with no hypothesis, may be more sensitive to accidental discoveries than those deliberately testing a precisely stated explanatory hypothesis. In addition, Sidman maintains that helpful experiments may be conducted to try out a new technique, or to see what kind of data would result from the use of a new technique.

"Hypothesis" as used in this monograph is not intended to exclude, but rather to include, what Sidman discusses. Surely the curiosity of a skilled and competent investigator is affected by the state of development of his discipline, current problems and controversies, etc. What would be regarded as a new or surprising discovery depends on the previous achievements in a given field. To test the notion that something worthy of scientific attention may

---

[22]Murray Sidman: *Tactics of Scientific Research: Evaluating Experimental Data in Psychology,* New York, Basic Books, 1960. This volume is written from the point of view of the practicing experimentalist. Although the present writer objects to the emphasis on the personal nature of science given by Sidman, Sidman's comments should be taken seriously by those methodologists of science with a formalistic bent.

result if such and such things are done is here considered as the testing of a hypothesis.

What are some of the possible merits of the highly theoretical writers? Perhaps of primary importance is their insistence on the relevance of theory, and their view that nonuse of theory frequently covers up a covert, uncriticized, and perhaps highly dubious theory. The particular norms prevalent in a given segment of humanity may have little or no evidence in support of them but yet function in an important way in the selection of problems, the consideration of "possible" alternatives, and the specific techniques thought to be usable. The social context is only too likely to supply working hypotheses for those who profess to need none. From the vantage point of hindsight, some very elaborate theoretical structures that at the time of their formulation had little prospect of verification have turned out to be significant indeed.

On the other hand, in extreme cases such as the insistence that some assumptions are beyond any experiential control or refutation, the excessive fear of allowing for such refutation can be perhaps best explained in clinical terms. A man of sufficient learning, ingenuity, and habits of hard work frequently can develop theories that, if doomed by laboratory results, can be modified in an *ad hoc* way so as to remain immune to refutation. Although certainly considerable flexibility in modifying hypotheses to accord with new evidence is a scientific virtue, on occasion it may shade into such flexibility that nothing can shake the hypothesis. Some of the frantic attempts to save the ether theory are illuminating in this connection.[23]

In contemporary writings curious happenings relate to the tendency to take as pan-human traits that may characterize only the members of one culture, or the members of one socioeconomic class. Various notions in economics, game theory, etc., about the maximizing of utility may be mentioned. If it is shown that some groups, or entire cultures, do not in fact act in a way conforming to the assumptions, the notion of utility is likely to be changed, refined, and in general made so complex that hardly anyone can say

---

[23]For an incisive commentary on some of the dangers of *ad hoc* hypotheses, see Mario Bunge: Cosmology and magic, *The Monist*, 1962, Vol. 47, sections 6, 7, and 8.

whether or not it does apply to most humans. But even if this is in-correct, and some economists have uncovered well-nigh universal springs of action, it seems odious to forever insist on their universal character. One would expect that the defenders of such views would search diligently for confirmation of their views and pay the greatest attention to apparently divergent groups. But the fear that unless certainty is achieved at the beginning, nothing further can be done, operates to force closure, and we meet with adamant statements that the assumptions do have pan-human applicability.

If specific contexts are kept in mind, it seems possible to describe in a straightforward and nontechnical way what the "proper" rela-tion is between hypotheses and laboratory confirmation. To begin with, the scientist initiates his inquiry under the influence of many factors, not the least of which is his social role. One might well wish that the passionate search for warranted assertions was uniformly institutionalized in behavioral inquirers. Very thoroughly institu-tionalized, however, is the spur to academic and professional ad-vancement, the desire for repute in the peer group, the need to take care of financial dependents, etc. Such factors may impose a near stranglehold on a discipline at a given place and time, and the views of deviants may be eliminated from serious consideration. So many highly significant scientific advances have occurred against the direction of the stream that one need not be heterodox to hint that approved modes of behavior do not always lead to scientific progress.

To return to our hypothetical scientist, he would not be human if his technical education had not opened some possibilities for him and closed others. He may have various ideological commitments that make some paths of inquiry unusually attractive, and getting certain results may make him especially happy. Previous progress (or lack of it) in research, as well as the technical facilities open to him, also indicate certain problems and foreclose others. He is guided by other presumably well-established findings. The in-quirer may begin with a clearly stated hypothesis, or he may begin with an intriguing problem and try to make some headway with it, or he may find the apparatus available to him interesting enough so that he tries to work out problems for which that apparatus is suited. He may begin with one hypothesis, find it boring and go on to another, or find so many technical obstacles to his work that he cannot proceed, or hit upon something in the course of his work that suggests a new problem, or a new hypothesis. Or, for that matter, he may begin with the aim of refuting someone else's theory, or some segment of that theory. Many other possible factors may be involved. In this whole process the running of experiments, the controlled collecting of data, etc., make sense in terms of possible predictions of behavior. No matter how delightful the theory, should it go glaringly against the evidence it will be finally discarded, even by the most ardent "pure" theorists. Massive collections of data that serve no useful purpose in testing hypotheses probably also will be allowed quietly to collect dust.

Judging by the most conspicuous scientific successes to date, it seems clear that in the main, and overall, the most desirable situation is that in which significant hypotheses amenable to relatively rigorous empirical testing are in fact tested, and the hypotheses then discarded, modified, or tentatively accepted in the light of the evidence. This is such a simple point it may be worthwhile to ask why it is sometimes disputed. One major reason is that the formal accounts of this process make it seem entirely too neat and tidy. One begins with "facts," but of course the actual situation is that the facts may be quite indefinite, and in the course of inquiry what previously were thought to be hard facts may turn out to be conspicuously erroneous. The development of better measuring devices may call into doubt some of the finer achievements of an earlier time. The consequences deduced from the hypothesis are sometimes discussed as if their selection posed no problems, whereas in view of how many consequences might be deduced from a given family of hypotheses (in conjunction with "established laws," etc.), principles of selectivity play a significant role.

It is not argued here that the theoretician and the laboratorian must be the same person. One suspects that such a union would be a pleasant event, should it occur, but since human interests, abilities, time, and energy are limited, far more frequently than not the two roles will be carried on by different people. Nor is it affirmed that all "respectable" hypotheses must be subject to current or near-future tests; nor that apparently insignificant compilations of data must be exorcised from science, inasmuch as a new theory may call for just that data. All that is asserted is that if, given always the context, there is not a close mutual relation between the two functions, the area of inquiry is not in a promising condition.

Again, if one does not focus attention exclusively on the more technical, formal, methodological issues, but keeps in mind the recent history of many of the disciplines and their position in our society, some otherwise baffling and/or peculiar statements make considerable sense. For example, the statement earlier quoted from Goldstein (that a theory will help the investigator find a solution if the theory is accurate, but that it will hinder the investigator if it is inaccurate) is obviously wrong, considered from one point of view. Many now rejected theories not only once were widely accepted, but helped the course of a science, as is illustrated in many concrete instances in physics. A wrong hypothesis may have logical consequences that are amply confirmed, and in that sense help solve at least minor problems. What, then, might Goldstein have in mind? A good guess is that he is thinking of cases in which a mistaken theory generated many problems which never would have been generated by the empirical situation, but flow instead from assumptions of the theory. This point of view is emphatically expressed by Norman Cameron, who after rejecting a mind-body dualism, says:

> "We begin instead with what we find, a biological organism operating in and by means of a social environment. We thus create no artificial need to solve such meaningless conundrums as, *How does the soma affect the psyche? How does the psyche influence the soma? And how is non-psychic reality ever contacted and tested by an insubstantial psyche?* The questions are not inherent in the problems which our patients present. They are the offspring of psychosomatic dualism and we can discard them with their parent."

> "We have already wasted years of effort in trying to work out the internal structure of a fictitious psyche and its esoteric love life, when we might better have been working out the dynamics of the organization, disorganization and reorganization of human behavior. . ."[24]

---

[24]Norman Cameron: *The Psychology of Behavior Disorders: A Biosocial Interpretation,* Boston, Houghton Mifflin, 1947, p. xx and p. xix.

Thus the kind of criticism being discussed may better be framed as a protest, not against mistaken hypotheses, but against hypotheses going so far beyond any actual testing as to yield a high probability that the problems investigated are not related to actual human behavior, but rather flow from purely theoretical considerations. And it is indeed striking to note the very many pleas in behavioral science literature that the theoretician and the laboratorian be brought closer together. Many representative statements can be cited;[25] the view of W. K. Estes will serve here as typical. He compares certain aspects of game theory and decision theory with some of the traditional deductive systems in ethics, and holds that in the study of human choices, "elaboration of theory has far outrun the front line of empirical investigation." He also argues that very frequently the inquirer in those areas first selects a certain theory that he prefers, and then looks for empirical support. Estes thinks there is a need to begin with the experimental data and introduce hypotheses to account for that data.[26]

To summarize this section, it has not been maintained that either highly theoretical work relatively unconnected with empirical research, or data collecting relatively unconnected with broad theoretical efforts, are necessarily always to be discouraged. Rather the simple point has been that in discipline after discipline, the behavioral areas are currently plagued by a disturbing gap between the theoretician and the laboratorian. In such situations it is natural to inquire into some of the reasons, and attention here has been given to the sociocultural context, with special emphasis on the notion that rewards to inquirers are often allotted with little regard for the testing of hypotheses. In this connection the views of the anthropologist, John Gillin, may be mentioned. He suggests that in our society scientists are rated on "individual distinction,"

[25]What seems to be a representative sampling of pleas for the closer rapport of theory and testing is contained in the following: Charles Gide and Charles Rist: *A History of Economic Doctrines*, 2nd English ed., Boston, Heath, 1948, p. 763; The 1954 report of the Committee on Historiography of the Social Science Research Council: *The Social Sciences in Historical Study*, New York, Social Science Research Council, Bulletin No. 64, 1954, pp. 136-38; Heinz Eulau, Samuel J. Eldersveld and Morris Janowitz: *op. cit.*, pp. 3-4.

[26]W. K. Estes: A descriptive approach to the dynamics of choice behavior, *Behavioral Science*, 6:178, 1961.

and competition is often the route available to win that distinction. The behavioral scientist, he goes on, is unlikely to achieve distinction measured in monetary terms, and often the goal becomes "being different from others." Gillin maintains that one result is the "cluttering" of the field with purposely, but not necessarily consciously, irreconcilable theories. Careers can be made of defending the theories, yet little or nothing may be achieved in the way of viable scientific conclusions.[27]

By this time, some readers may have become impatient with the preceding discussion and want specific examples. Therefore the next section is devoted to an account of some of the developments in the *newer* areas of behavioral science. The purpose of the section is to help illustrate why one finds so many pleas for bringing together the theoretician and the laboratorian.

9. SOME EXAMPLES OF THE FAILURE TO UNITE THEORY AND LABORATORY WORK[28]

Certain aspects of game theory are of special interest in this connection. Some regard game theory as a revolutionary "breakthrough," and it has been favorably compared to Newtonian achievements. R. Duncan Luce and Howard Raiffa mention that some authors felt the theory either solved "innumerable" problems in economics and sociology, or at least "made their solution a practical matter of a few years' work."[29] Before going further, we may specifically mention one recurring phenomenon. The understandable enthusiasm of workers in a new area is only too likely to lead to exaggerated notions of what has been, or what can be, achieved. This would not necessarily be troublesome if sufficient attention were given to empirical testing. But if the climate of opinion does not call for thorough testing, the unwarranted enthusiasm and exaggeration may continue to grow, and if the testing

[27]John Gillin, ed.: *For a Science of Social Man*, New York, Macmillan, 1954, pp. 275-76.

[28]Some of the material in this section is adapted from Rollo Handy and Paul Kurtz: *A Current Appraisal of the Behavioral Sciences*, Great Barrington, Mass., Behavioral Research Council, 1964. For a fuller discussion, see Chs. X, XIII, XIV, and XVI of that volume.

[29]R. Duncan Luce and Howard Raiffa: *Games and Decisions*, New York, Wiley, 1957, p. 10.

finally is performed and the theory shows up poorly, the resulting disillusionment may also serve to blind one to possible merits of the approach in question.

What then helps to account for the initial enthusiasm? Here we immediately encounter another problem. Some of the newer areas call for such specialized knowledge that a nontechnical account is likely to be severely misleading. But one of the major hopes of game theory was to offer a much more precise and manageable approach to questions which traditionally have been troublesome. Presumably no one would deny that many forms of human behavior are at least partly analogous to the playing of games that involve both possible cooperation with partners and competition among players. If the conditions of the game are known, and if certain assumptions are made about the behavior of the players, the conditions under which the player has the best chance of maximizing his "pay-off" can be stated.

Without doubt much ability and ingenuity have gone into the solution of a variety of games. One could have wished for equally conscientious consideration of how analogous human behavior is to the kind of behavior assumed in the games. Quite often those working in game theory had relatively little acquaintance with relevant findings in the social sciences, and may have been prone to assume characteristics of human behavior that at best are dubious and at worst systematically wrong. As mentioned earlier, in some disciplines there has been a long tradition of beginning with certain alleged universal human traits and taking them as well-founded enough so they need not be tested. The influence of traditional economic theory on game theory probably lent much support to that tendency. The strong emphasis on the notion of "utility," and the theories developed on that basis, have often been criticized. For example, in an impressive attempt to relate experimental psychology to economics, C. Reinold Noyes argues that much of marginal utility theory simply is inconsistent with well-supported psychological findings.[30] Even if Noyes is wrong, it certainly seems

---

[30] C. Reinold Noyes: *Economic Man in Relation to His Natural Environment*, 2 vols., New York, Columbia University Press, 1948. See, for example, Vol. 1, p. 227 and Vol. 2, pp. 1372 ff. and p. 1408.

unhealthy that so much work could have been based on marginal utility considerations without seeing what bearing other social science findings might have on the issue.

John von Neumann and Oskar Morgenstern say some interesting things about their work in game theory. Their hope was to show that "the typical problems of economic behavior become strictly identical with the mathematical notions of suitable games of strategy." They also clearly indicated that their interests were in the elaboration of the theory, not in direct empirical research. They were fully aware that the mere mathematical formulation of a theory need be no improvement over a literary formulation, and point out that much dissatisfaction with mathematicized economic theory is just that questionable assertions given mathematical form remain questionable. In discussing their theory as a model for human behavior, they emphasize that models must be precise, yet not too complicated, and also be "similar to reality."[31] Yet as their work progresses, one suspects that the "similarity to reality" aspect yields to a concern for technical problems in the internal development of the theory. Thus they say that their treatment of the notion of "utility" is "rather narrow and dogmatic." They assumed "utility" to be numerical, and think that fairly good evidence can be cited in support of that. They also assumed that it is substitutable and unrestrictedly transferable between the players, which is much more doubtful. Why was this done? For technical reasons, since numerical utilities were needed for solving some games, and the substitutability and transferability notions were necessary for other games. They hoped that a generalization of their notion of "utility" could be developed, but foresaw many difficulties.[32]

There need be no objection to any of the above procedures, and the candor of the authors is admirable. However, users of game theory often fail to show similar caution about the applicability of their results, and questionable assumptions are frequently not questioned at all. Some of the problems relating to "rational" behavior and "utility" become intricate indeed. In game theory,

---

[31]John von Neumann and Oskar Morgenstern: *Theory of Games and Economic Behavior*, 3rd ed., Princeton, Princeton University Press, 1953, pp. 1–5, p. 32.

[32]*Ibid.*: p. 604.

rationality is often construed in terms of the maximizing of some quantity, the "utility." But pinning down the behavioral referent of "utility" is often difficult; it may be easier to find a snark.

Thus Luce and Raiffa emphasize that the individual's utility function should not be taken as identical with the numerical measure used in a specific game. They mention poker, and point out that although one way to play poker is to try to maximize the dollar winnings, players may also choose to play for the sake of bluffing, and their bluffing may have little relation to expected dollar pay-off.[33] Rapoport points out that in some situations "mathematical expectation" is clearly not the deciding factor. His example is the person taking out fire insurance. The mathematical expectation of such a person is negative, or insurance companies would go bankrupt.[34] And indeed many persons may operate on the basis of probability estimates that differ from mathematical probability. This is taken account of in some studies by introducing "subjective probability," which allows the application of game theory to such instances.

This is not to assert that something corresponding to "utility" in the sense necessary for a given theory cannot be found in human behavior. Rather it is to argue that before one assumes that game theory affords great new insight into human behavior, considerable testing is in order to ascertain just how behavior is interpretable in the light of those utilities. But even on the assumption that the utilities can be found, another general assumption causes grievous difficulties. Game theory assumed that the individuals know in full the utilities that the other players are attempting to maximize; i.e., every player is fully informed of the preference patterns of all the other players.[35] Since this is so clearly not the case in most human transactions, whether formally games or not, one would think that much testing is desirable to ascertain the extent to which those transactions do approximate what is assumed in the theory.

In view of the factors just described, and others, it is not surprising that a recent tendency is to deny that game theory is a descrip-

[33]Luce and Raiffa: *op. cit.*, p. 5.

[34]Anatol Rapoport: Introduction, in Dorothy Willner, ed.: *Decisions, Values, and Groups*, New York, Pergamon Press, 1960, Vol. 1, p. xv.

[35]Luce and Raiffa: *op. cit.*, p. 5.

tion of human behavior, and to find it defended rather as a pre-
scription of how a "rational" player should behave. Patrick Suppes
and Richard Atkinson, for example, report that predictions based
on game theory were not successful in the experiments they conducted, and conclude that it is not promising to take game theory
as a description of behavior.[36] Certainly many of the activities
carried on under the label of game theory make more sense if their
aim is viewed as prescriptive rather than descriptive. But if so, some
of the former claims that game theory marks a genuine breakthrough in the behavioral sciences are extremely wide of the mark.

Much of the work currently being done in decision theory relies
heavily on game theory. However, "decision theory" is also used to
refer to some relatively nonformalized work done on actual decision making processes. Emphasis is here placed on the more
formalized aspects of decision theory. Perhaps even more than in
the case of game theory, there is a difference of opinion as to
whether decision theory is descriptive or prescriptive. Sidney
Schoeffler, for example, regards it as remarkable that the principles
of decision making used by most people today are practically the
same as those of 2000 years ago. He suggests that decision theory,
game theory, operations research, modern logic, welfare economics, etc., can lead to more effective decision making.[37] Donald
Davidson, Patrick Suppes, and Sidney Siegel argue that many
models used in decision theory are defective since a satisfactory
empirical interpretation for them has not been given. They attempt to develop models for which such interpretations can be
given, but go on to say that even if decision theories have little
descriptive relevance, they still may have great "normative"
interest.[38] What may be a fairly typical result is reported by them.
Fifteen out of nineteen subjects, under controlled conditions, made
"choices among risky alternatives as if they were attempting to
maximize expected utility even when they do not make choices in

[36]Patrick Suppes and Richard C. Atkinson: *Markov Learning Models for Multiperson Interactions*, Stanford, Stanford University Press, 1960, p. 33.

[37]Sidney Schoeffler: *The Failures of Economics: A Diagnostic Study*, Cambridge, Harvard University Press, 1955, pp. 159-60.

[38]Donald Davidson, Patrick Suppes and Sidney Siegel: *Decision Making: An Experimental Approach*, Stanford, Stanford University Press, 1957, p. 3.

accord with actuarial values."[39] Alvin Scodel, Philburn Ratoosh, and J. Sayer Minas reported that in an experiment concerning gambling with dice, the expected dollar value had "negligible importance" in the determination of the betting preferences, and also that the subjects with information on probabilities and expected values were not any more likely to maximize expected dollar values than other subjects.[40]

Although there still seems to be considerable enthusiasm about the merits of formal decision theory, doubts have also been expressed. C. West Churchman, for example, argues that pure formalization seems about the last thing we should do, rather than the first, in decision theory. He emphasizes the need for reaching agreement on how observable behavior relates to the formal model, and suggests that in many respects formal decision theory is *not* a foundation for a theory of decisions.[41] In another place he criticizes the reliance of some model builders on "intuition," and maintains that just when a statement has the "clear support" of intuition we need to doubt it and subject it to analysis.[42]

In cybernetics and general systems theory the major problem seems to center on analogies. The discovery of an analogy between human behavior and the behavior of some other system (whether computer, solar system, meteorological system, etc.) makes some inquirers quite convinced that a revolutionary step forward either has been taken or is about to be taken. But, as often happens, the initial enthusiasm may be followed by disillusionment.[43] And many, if not most, criticisms of the attempts to explain human behavior by the cyberneticists and general systems theorists relate to what the critics see as an unjustifiable reliance on weak analogies. Before exploring the issue, it may be noted that workers in both fields are animated by a great desire to pursue interdisciplinary

[39]*Ibid.*: pp. 80-81.

[40]Alvin Scodel, Philburn Ratoosh and J. Sayer Minas: Some personality correlates of decision making under conditions of risk, in D. Willner, ed.: *op. cit.*, p. 48.

[41]C. West Churchman: Problems of value measurement for a theory of induction and decisions, *Proceedings of the Third Berkeley Symposium on Mathematical Statistics*, Berkeley, University of California Press, 1955, p. 55.

[42]C. West Churchman: *Prediction and Optimal Decision*, Englewood Cliffs, N. J., Prentice-Hall, 1961, p. 329.

[43]For example, see Caxton Foster's comments along these lines in his review of W. Ross Ashby's *An Introduction to Cybernetics*, in *Behavioral Science*, 2:319, 1957.

investigations, to help unify the behavioral and other sciences, to adopt a strictly scientific approach, and to bring areas sometimes considered as unamenable to scientific treatment into the scientific fold.[44]

To specify clearly and adequately what the fields of cybernetics and general systems theory include does not seem possible. Both areas are not only new, but in a state of rapid development that makes for understandable difficulties. Also characteristic of new fields is an imperialistic tendency to encompass an enormous array of fields. For example, Norbert Wiener was fond of defining "cybernetics" as including the entire field of communication theory, and as a general theory of control.[45] Sometimes the major focus of research is on feedback phenomena, and cyberneticists hold as a major hypothesis that negative feedback explains purposive and adaptive behavior.[46] Sometimes the emphasis is put on a comparative study of the control systems of the nervous system and that of mechanical electrical communication systems.[47] But in any event, much of the excitement and much of the actual work done in relating machine processes to human behavior concerns the finding of analogies between the two types of phenomena.

The same interest in analogies, often called "structural isomorphisms," or "formal identities," pervades general systems research. Anatol Rapoport, for example, has been excited over the fact that similar mathematical models can be developed for the spread of neural impulses, rumors, and epidemics.[48] John W. Thompson has noticed analogies between meteorology and psychology that he thinks may be significant.[49] James G. Miller has

---

[44]For example, see the various *Transactions* of the different American Conferences on Cybernetics, Josiah Macy, Jr., Foundation, New York; the various volumes of the yearbook, *General Systems;* and James G. Miller's Introduction in *Chicago Behavioral Sciences Publications*, No. 1, Profits and problems of homeostatic models in the behavioral sciences, Chicago, n.d.

[45]Norbert Wiener: *Cybernetics*, New York, John Wiley, 1948, p. 19.

[46]J. O. Wisdom: The hypothesis of cybernetics, *General Systems*, 1:112, 1956.

[47]F. H. George: *Automation, Cybernetics and Society*, New York, Philosophical Library, 1959, p. 45.

[48]Anatol Rapoport: Some mathematical models of the spread of information through a population, *Chicago Behavioral Sciences Publications*, No. 1, pp. 19-23.

[49]John W. Thompson: Mental science, meteorology, and general system theory, *General Systems*, 5:21, 1960.

written of the work of Ralph Gerard and the discovering of analogies between the behavior of the slime mold and the way humans behave under the stress of enemy attack.[50] James G. Miller has also listed nineteen systems hypotheses that are empirically testable at "the levels of cell, organ, individual, small group and society."[51]

Some general systems inquirers take as their task the formulation of principles that hold for all systems, of whatever kind. This immediately leads to a problem, since the task of specifying a "system" is troublesome. A frequently encountered view is that a system is a set of objects or elements and the relationships among those elements and among their attributes. Yet some adopting that view worry about freakish or ridiculous systems that they would like to exclude, but which are in accord with the above specification. That type of difficulty may be regarded as a healthy development in the early stage of a new field of inquiry. The only objection raised here is that sometimes enthusiastic proponents of general systems theory seem to forget the many problems confronting them, and believe they have made more progress than the evidence warrants.

Perhaps the major line of criticism encountered in the literature is that an uncritical attitude is often held about the analogies. Far too often, it seems to the critics, the mere discovery of the analogy is taken as having great significance, and unreasonably high hopes are held for what will be found when the analogies are tested. Probably the most hostile critic along these lines is R. C. Buck.[52] Again, there can be no objection to a time lag between the elaboration of a hypothesis and its testing, nor should it be denied that very often the discovery of an analogy may prove most helpful in furthering scientific progress. What is objected to is the apparent confidence some have that the mere stating of the analogy will lead to scientific advance.

Some of the older behavioral fields, as we have seen, contain workers who deal with theories that seem impossible to test, or have

---

[50] James G. Miller in *Chicago Behavioral Sciences Publications*, No. 1, pp. 8-9.

[51] James G. Miller: Toward a general theory for the behavioral sciences, *The American Psychologist*, 10:525, 1955.

[52] R. C. Buck: On the logic of general behavior systems theory, in H. Feigl and M. Scriven, eds.: *Minnesota Studies in the Philosophy of Science*, Minneapolis, University of Minnesota Press, 1956, Vol. 1.

workers who deny the relevance of testing. General systems and cybernetics researchers, on the other hand, in the main want to develop testable hypotheses and assiduously avoid any intrinsically untestable theories. But on the other hand, the extensive elaboration of theory beyond actual or foreseen testing makes a situation ripe for pernicious overemphasis on theory. And, on occasion, we have in the guise of a hard science inquiry the most naive and uncritical metaphysical speculation.[53] To take an extreme case, consider the following quotation from Ludwig von Bertalanffy, the father of general systems theory:

> "The world is, as Aldous Huxley once put it, like a Neapolitan ice cake where the levels, the physical, the biological, the social and moral universe, represent the chocolate, strawberry, and vanilla layers. We cannot reduce strawberry to chocolate—the most we can say is that possibly in the last resort, all is vanilla, all mind or spirit."[54]

In addition a state of affairs frequently found in the new areas of behavioral science is also found here. Initial assumptions, if clearly stated at all, are forgotten about when the areas to which the theory is to be applied are considered. This exacerbates the overgeneralization of possible results and may tend to obscure genuine merit.[55]

Doubts have also been expressed as to the value of those analogies, formal identities, etc., that in fact do hold. May Brodbeck has argued this point, using as her example all the many types of things that can be ranked and measured. All of these have the same "structure" as arithmetical addition, and hence "structural isomorphisms" run through all those types, including arithmetic. She goes on to say that only the isomorphism with arithmetic may be significant, and there may be no connection of the kind envisaged in general systems among all the things isomorphic to arithmetic.[56]

[53]See, for example, the comments by Buck: *op. cit.*, p. 226.

[54]Ludwig von Bertalanffy: General system theory, *General Systems*, *1*:8, 1956.

[55]See, on this point, Russell L. Ackoff: Games, decisions, and organizations, *General Systems*, *IV*: especially p. 145, 1959.

[56]May Brodbeck: Models, meaning and theories, in Dorothy Willner, ed.: *op. cit.*, p. 28. For a good brief account of the role of analogies in developing hypotheses, see Harold A. Larrabee: *Reliable Knowledge*, rev. ed., Boston, Houghton Mifflin, 1964, pp. 137-40.

Although many more examples of the above phenomena could be cited, perhaps enough have been given to illustrate why so many people have greeted the alleged new breakthroughs with something approaching derision. Until and unless the requisite testing program is instituted, it is always possible for some to maintain hope for revolutionary progress from the new approaches. In at least a few cases, this hope may produce an unconscious motive for not putting more emphasis on testing. But perhaps most important of all is the unwarranted shift from consideration of possible future achievements that will conform to the usual scientific criteria, to the view that such achievements have already occurred.

In order to avoid possible misunderstanding, it may be useful to state that the present writer has no ideological, philosophical, or other prejudices against cybernetics or any other approach attempting to view all human behavior scientifically. Indeed, such ideological prejudices as he has are in the direction of viewing "man as a machine." The objection to much that has been done in these areas, then, is not that it demeans man, etc., but rather that such grandiose claims have been made with so little warrant. The present writer expects that many cybernetic hypotheses will in fact turn out to be well supported, and hence has all the more reason to want to see these warrants developed.

10. A FINAL WORD

A highly annoying complication results from the widely differing kinds of terminology often used in discussions of issues relevant to this chapter. Not only do people using similar terminology sometimes disagree strongly, but what appear to be enormous differences in point of view, judging by the language used, sometimes turn out to be minor. To illustrate the latter case, some of Mario Bunge's comments will be discussed. Bunge refers to a kind of "distance" or "gap" between constructs and percepts, and mentions "transcendent or transempirical concepts" that lack ostensive referents, such as " 'conductivity,' 'randomness,' 'violence,' and 'love.' "[57] In the present monograph, in contrast, "concept," "transcendent,"

---

[57]Mario Bunge: *The Myth of Simplicity*, Englewood Cliffs, N. J., Prentice-Hall, 1963, p. 71.

and "transempirical" are avoided, and constant reference is made to the link between terms used, theories, etc., and empirical observation.

It might seem, then, that Bunge's view is in strong opposition to that of the present author, and that whether or not science uses "transempirical concepts" is a major question. Yet Bunge's account of ways of avoiding useless multiplication of scientific constructs seems to be just what is advocated here (although in different language) when the union of theoretical and laboratory work is urged:

> "Firstly, every construct, however high its order of mediacy (remoteness from sense-data), must somehow somewhere be related, by means of correspondence rules (e.g., coordinative definitions) and law statements, to lower-order concepts. Secondly, constructs must ultimately be incorporated in testable theories. (Terms such as 'superego' and 'telepathy' are not objected to because they are transempirical but because they do not occur in testable theories.) Thirdly, conceptual entities should not be multiplied *in vain* (Occam's razor); but they should be welcomed whenever they lead either to a deeper understanding of reality or to a syntactical simplification of theories. In this respect, science seems to take a middle course between the poverty of phenomenalism and the waste of transcendentalism."[58]

In short, how broadly "empirical" is used may be a basic consideration. The present essay uses that term to include what Bunge and others call "transcendent." A genuine difference may be that Bunge apparently thinks what is (in the narrow sense) observable or has an ostensive referent is "safer" than I do; recent work in perception (referred to in Chapter III and elsewhere) makes that safety illusory. Avoiding a sharp separability between so-called "percepts" and "concepts," then, characterizes the present approach, and with that avoidance goes a rejection of some lines of differentiation between the empirical and the transcendent.

---

[58]*Ibid.:* p. 75.

3

TRANSACTION, INTERACTION, SELF-ACTION

1. BACKGROUND AND COMPLEXITY OF ISSUES

ALTHOUGH the words in this chapter's title may not be used as often as some others relating to the general problem to be discussed, the problem itself occurs in many of the behavioral fields. For example, from time to time atomistic approaches are rejected in favor of organismic or neo-organismic approaches. The development of a unified scientific framework in general systems theory, to mention a recent case, was stimulated by neo-organismic notions in opposition to the type of analysis characteristic of logical positivism.[1] Atomism vs. holism is a controversy cropping up again and again; psychology seems an especially fertile ground for such disputes. Not only have gestaltists protested an overemphasis on the parts making up a whole, but many others have objected to extreme behavioristic reductionism.[2] Historically many dialectical or neodialectical theories have been advocated in place of mechanistic theories. *Analytic vs. synthetic, dialectical vs. mechanical*, and *atomistic vs. holistic* are only a few of the labels for controversies frequently encountered. Of course many different issues have been debated in those disputes, but there are also some common themes.

As the previous paragraph suggests, sometimes those disputes stem largely from disagreements about basic philosophic positions. But even if many of those urging a synthetic rather than an analytic method have idealistic philosophic inclinations, and their opponents naturalistic or positivistic inclinations, to regard the battle as one between the *tough* and the *tender* minded, or as between idealists and naturalists, would be mistaken. Norman Cameron's

---

[1]See the editors' preface to Vol. 7, *General Systems*, 1962.

[2]See, for example, the recent paper by Rex M. Collier: A holistic-organismic theory of consciousness, *Journal of Individual Psychology*, *19*, 1963. Collier attempts to rescue 'consciousness' for scientific work, and strives to avoid both dualism and mechanistic reduction.

psychological theory, referred to earlier, is strikingly tough minded, and yet he makes a special point of emphasizing the holistic nature of his theory.[3] And Dewey and Bentley's transactionalism criticizes logical positivists for retaining too many mysterious and sometimes mentalistic elements.[4]

The general dispute becomes even more complicated, in that methodological, substantive, and sometimes ideological issues are mixed together. To illustrate, let us consider in some detail the recent literature on "methodological individualism." Although the term has been used in different ways, the core doctrine seems to be that *social* phenomena are to be investigated, understood, and explained as the outcome of the actions of the *individuals* making up the social group in question.[5] Sometimes support for such a methodology is linked to a defense of free-enterprise capitalism and hostility to governmental control over the economy, as in the case of F. A. Hayek.[6] However, that methodology is also sometimes advocated by those of welfare state or even socialistic predilections. Hayek is mentioned not as evidence that one's social views necessarily affect one's methodological views, but rather to illustrate some of the complex configurations of belief encountered in this area.

Although often methodological problems are primarily at issue in the various controversies about methodological individualism, substantive issues may also be involved; the most basic being the question of the extent to which the "individual" and the "social" are empirically separable. Supporters of methodological individual-

---

[3]Norman Cameron: *The Psychology of Behavior Disorders: A Biosocial Interpretation*, Boston, Houghton Mifflin, 1947, Preface.

[4]John Dewey and Arthur F. Bentley: *Knowing and the Known*, Boston, Beacon Press, 1949, especially Ch. I.

[5]See, for example, Patrick Suppes and Franklin Krasne: Application of stimulus sampling theory to situations involving social pressure, *Psychological Review*, 68, 1961. In his helpful article, Methodological and epistemological individualism, *British Journal for the Philosophy of Science*, XI, 1961, K. J. Scott distinguishes between F. A. Hayek's methodological individualism (the data in social science are the relations between individual minds that we know directly) and Karl Popper's epistemological individualism (whatever methods are used, we should not accept explanations in terms of "collectives" such as states, nations, etc.). Many recent supporters of methodological individualism seem to combine both notions, and perhaps others.

[6]F. A. Hayek: *The Counter-Revolution of Science: Studies on the Abuse of Reason*, Glencoe, Ill., Free Press, 1952.

ism sometimes use their theory primarily to protest against the hypostatization of "society," "group," or other collective terms, and at other times argue that the most effective way to study group behavior is to "construct" it out of individual behavior. A major difficulty with many of the controversies over methodological individualism is confusion as to just what is at issue. Once certain ideological and other relatively extraneous elements are purged, it is not always clear whether the battle is about the most effective technique of inquiry, the most adequate form of explanation, or the existence of certain entities.

A roughly parallel case from mechanics may be helpful. Assume that accurate prediction of the motions of all the molecules of a cannon ball is possible, and that the resultant of the motions of all those molecules is equivalent to the motion of the whole cannon ball. In such a case, it would be possible to "reduce" the behavior of the whole to the behavior of the parts, but it would be an inefficient and cumbersome way of predicting the path of the cannon ball. Sometimes critics of methodological individualism seem to be making a fairly similar point: although the reduction of group to individual behavior may be theoretically possible, to carry out such reduction would impede inquiry into the group processes, for better and quicker techniques are available. In some cases, although it seems obvious that the group phenomenon is a resultant of individual actions, the behavior of the group can be predicted much more accurately than that of the items making it up. For example, actuarial studies may be highly accurate in predicting the number of people in a certain group who will die in a certain year, even though to predict individual cases would be far more difficult and inaccurate.

On the other hand, sometimes mysterious properties are said to inhere in groups that are not explainable in terms of the parts of the group *and* the relations among them. One suspects that sometimes methodological individualists are trying to eliminate such mysticism and to point out dangerous reifications.

In the last few years some writers have become suspicious of recent discussions of the controversy. K. J. Scott, for example, says of much of the recent work: "the game's not worth the candle."[7]

---

[7]Scott: *op. cit.*, p. 331.

Some dissatisfaction with the whole dispute may stem from the proclivity of many to look for methodological rules they can accept almost absolutely and use to thwart their opponents *a priori*. A more pragmatic approach may be desirable; namely to use the rules and tools that lead to successful inquiry. Sometimes a more holistic method, sometimes a less, may be the most effective, depending upon the problem at hand. Probably of far more significance in actual inquiry than the question as to whether some given group behavior can be "reduced" to individual behaviors is the question of the degree to which a given individual behavior pattern is socialized. We so easily assume as universal behavior what in fact varies from person to person, class to class, and culture to culture, that assuming an unwarranted universality may often be a major problem. In any event, the question of how holistic an approach should be adopted is settled more appropriately in terms of success or failure of predictions, etc., than in terms of epistemological issues only marginally relevant to actual inquiry.

2. PRESENT FOCUS OF ATTENTION

Many of the above issues that seem of considerable importance for behavioral science areas are related to John Dewey and A. F. Bentley's discussion of *transaction, interaction,* and *self-action*.[8] Recently some behavioral scientists, especially in psychology, sociology, and political science, have made conscious use of the Dewey-Bentley transactionalism, and other workers have adopted a similar view. The use of the Dewey-Bentley approach in some areas of behavioral science, and its basic importance, justify centering attention on it in this chapter. Dewey and Bentley give the following preliminary account of the three terms:

"*Self-Action:* where things are viewed as acting under their own powers.

"*Inter-action:* where thing is balanced against thing in causal inter-connection.

"*Trans-action:* where systems of description and naming are employed to deal with aspects and phases of action, without final attribution to 'elements' or other presumptively detachable or

---

[8]Dewey and Bentley: *op. cit.*, Chapters IV and V.

independent 'entities,' 'essences,' or 'realities,' and without isolation of presumptively detachable 'relations' from such detachable 'elements.' "[9]

3. SELF-ACTION

Dewey and Bentley argue that at one time self-action approaches dominated physics: "It took Jupiter Pluvius to produce a rainstorm for the early Romans, whereas modern science takes its *pluvius* free from Jupiter." They mention as terms that reek of self-action: "substance," "entity," "essence," "actor," "creator," "cause," etc.[10] They argue that Galileo's approach marked the overthrow of self-action in physics.

Something parallel, in important respects, to self-action in physics is often adopted in the behavioral sciences. Sociologists and others, for example, are fond of working out actor-action schemes. And indeed much of what is called "philosophical psychology" stresses the same thing, not to mention psychology without the qualifier. Many today who maintain that the social sciences can be scientific, but not in the way the physical sciences are, put emphasis on motives, intentions, purposes, etc.[11]

Self-action approaches lend themselves easily to mind-body, man-nature, man-animal, etc., divisions, bifurcations, dichotomies and separations. One suspects that most humans find few doctrines as gratifying as one giving man some obviously superior cosmic status. Human pride, rather than success in inquiry, may well turn out to be a major factor in the perpetuation of and insistence on a self-actional mode of interpreting human behavior. Tradition, also, not to mention superstition, is an enormously potent factor. A body-spirit dualism is so entrenched in our civilization that it is understandable and perhaps pardonable that many find it hard to give up, even on a tentative, trial basis. One may also observe the great confidence of many that adequate explanations of human be-

[9]*Ibid.:* p. 108.

[10]*Ibid.:* p. 110.

[11]For example, Robert Brown, in his recent book, *Explanation in Social Science*, Chicago, Aldine, 1963, argues that good scientific explanations occur in the social sciences, but also emphasizes that "only in the social sciences" do "explanations in terms of purposes, motives, intentions, and reasons have any place." (Pp. 3-4.)

havior are possible when couched in terms of intentions, etc. Very often these days philosophers, who can hardly contain pride in their sophistication relative to the "crudities" of the behavioral scientists, protest against the natural science trend in the behavioral sciences, and take as granted the superiority of explanations in terms of motives and intentions.[12] Perhaps such sophisticates would do well to consider the point raised by Wesley Mitchell, the institutional economist, in 1925, when he maintained that far from constituting satisfactory explanations, motives themselves need to be explained scientifically.[13]

In addition to the factors mentioned above, it may be that linguistic factors also are important in perpetuating the self-actional view. Leonard Bloomfield, for example, insisted that many structural features of English that we assume are universal, including the actor-action sentence, are in fact not so, and are peculiarities of Indo-European languages.[14]

Perhaps it is worth emphasizing that the present author is not trying to eliminate self-action assumptions from social science inquiries. As always, the view here upheld is that the approach best facilitating the inquiry at hand should be adopted. For limited purposes and in specific contexts no harm may be done by relying on an actor-action framework, and indeed that framework may sometimes be the most economical and efficient for arriving at warranted assertions. But the actor-action framework can also hinder other inquiries, and to assume it provides a universal framework for all inquiry can be extremely dangerous. Not only may it tend to

---

[12]An interesting and to some extent typical expression of this point of view can be found in Raziel Abelson's review of A. I. Melden's *Free Action*, in *Philosophy and Phenomenological Research*, *XXIII*:616-17, 1963. Abelson regards the series of monographs on philosophical psychology, of which Melden's book is a part, as a major revolution. He adds that "devotees of natural science will regard this development as more of a counter-revolution," and goes on to say that the generalizations of psychologists and sociologists "seem either hopelessly vague or hopelessly banal." In his opinion, "novelists, journalists, and historians seem able to explain human conduct with far more insight than psychologists and sociologists."

[13]Wesley C. Mitchell: Quantitative analysis in economic theory, *American Economic Review*, *XV*, 1925.

[14]Leonard Bloomfield: Linguistic aspects of science, *International Encyclopedia of Unified Science*, Chicago, University of Chicago, 1955, Vol. 1, No. 4. Originally published in 1939.

detach the "mental" aspect of the human biosocial organism from the remainder of the organism, but it may lead to an underestimation of some factors influencing human behavior. One more qualification is appropriate here: it is not asserted that the mere use of self-action terminology in and of itself leads to undesirable results or the hampering of inquiry. Both the language and the method may be useful; the dangers result from overgeneralization and the failure to realize the limitations of the language system and the method.

4. INTERACTION

Although the present writer believes that Dewey and Bentley draw a clear distinction between *transactions* and *interactions*, it should be observed that some contemporary writers use the terminology of *interaction* to describe what Dewey and Bentley call transaction. J. R. Kantor's interactional psychology, for example, has many important similarities to transactionalism, and Hadley Cantril and William K. Livingston point out that "few dictionaries and few individuals make any fundamental distinction between transaction and interaction."[15]

Dewey and Bentley say that *interaction* "furnished the dominant pattern of scientific procedure up to the beginning of the last generation," and that its very successes resulted in many imitations and debasements that now require modification. They differentiate four types of interactional patterns: 1) those such as Newtonian mechanics that still work efficiently; 2) inquiries provisionally given interactional form with the recognition, however, that the results are subject to reinterpretation in wider systems, such as the investigation of interactions of tissues and organs; 3) abuses of the first, as when "efforts were made to force all knowledge under the mechanistic control of the Newtonian system"; and 4) grosser abuses such as when "minds and portions of matter in separate realms are brought by the epistemologies into pseudo-interactional forms."[16]

---

[15]J. R. Kantor: *Psychology and Logic*, Bloomington, Ind., Principia Press, 1945, Vol. I, 1950, Vol. II. Hadley Cantril and William K. Livingston: The concept of transaction in psychology and neurology, *Journal of Individual Psychology*, 19:4, 1963.

[16]Dewey and Bentley: *op. cit.*, pp. 108-9.

Although Dewey and Bentley have many words of praise for Newtonian mechanics, they also argue that such a closed system pays the price of important omissions. It took a near revolution for physicists to get beyond the Newtonian framework, and the unalterability of Newtonian particles was an "omission" of some importance. The giving up of Newtonian ideas proceeded along transactional lines, according to Dewey and Bentley, and involved "the seeing together, when research requires it, of what before had been seen in separations and held severally apart." Yet again a certain tolerance is advocated:

> "Our assertion is the right to see in union what it becomes important to see in union; together with the right to see in separation what it is important to see in separation—each in its own time and place. . . ."[17]

5. TRANSACTIONALISM

Dewey and Bentley are especially anxious to avoid "any form of hypostatized underpinning" for their transactionalism. They insist that any admissable statement about a knower, mind, self, subject, known thing, object, etc., has to be made "on the basis, and in terms, of aspects of events which inquiry . . . finds taking place."[18] They also emphasize that all existing descriptions of events are tentative and subject to modification or rejection at any stage of inquiry.[19]

A lengthy quotation may be helpful:

> "If we watch a hunter with his gun go into a field where he sees a small animal already known to him by name as a rabbit, then, within the framework of half an hour and an acre of land, it is easy —and for immediate purposes satisfactory enough—to report the shooting that follows in an interactional form in which rabbit and hunter and gun enter as separates and come together by way of cause and effect. If, however, we take enough of the earth and enough thousands of years, and watch the identification of rabbit gradually taking place, arising first in the sub-naming processes of gesture, cry, and attentive movement, wherein both rabbit and

[17]*Ibid.:* p. 112.
[18]*Ibid.:* p. 121.
[19]*Ibid.:* p. 122.

hunter participate, and continuing on various levels of description and naming, we shall soon see the transactional account as the one that best covers the ground ... No one would be able successfully to speak of the hunt*er* and the hunt*ed* as isolated with respect to hunt*ing*. Yet it is just as absurd to set up hunt*ing* as an event in isolation from the spatio-temporal connection of all the components."

Or again they maintain:

"Borrower cannot borrow without lender to lend, nor lender lend without borrower to borrow, the loan being a transaction that is identifiable only in the wider transaction of the full legal-commercial system in which it is present as occurrence."[20]

Perhaps, then, *transaction* can be taken as designating the full ongoing process in a field where the connections among the aspects and phases of the field and the inquirer himself are in common process. No mysticism should be attached to "field"; it here names a cluster of connected things and events as found by inquirers. Fields are brought in, not to ape various developments in physics, but because inquiry shows that emphasis on presumed self-actors or separates in interaction does not suffice. Better predictions result from an emphasis on the whole transaction.

This hostility to dualism is recognised by Dewey and Bentley as having some kinship to traditional objective idealism. Dewey and Bentley see some merits in the idealistic emphasis on "a full system of activity," etc., but maintain that their own approach "in contrast, is of the earth earthy, representing strictly an interest in improved methods of research, for whatever they are worth here and now."[21]

6. SOME EPISTEMOLOGICAL CONSEQUENCES

Dewey and Bentley have many harsh things to say about traditional epistemologies. A major current of their attack is the tendency to separate what is best viewed in union. They think their view, compared to customary theories of knowledge, has obvious superiorities with respect to what is observable. For example, who

---

[20]Both quotations *Ibid.:* p. 133.
[21]*Ibid.:* Note 7, pp. 139-40.

could claim properly that he can observe a "mind" in addition to the organism engaged in transactions? Similarly, who can observe objects entirely outside of or apart from human operations? They continue:

> "Observation is operation; it is human operation. If attributed to a 'mind' it itself becomes unobservable. If surveyed in an observable world—in what we call cosmos or nature—the object observed is as much a part of the operation as is the observing organism."[22]

Putting the matter another way, although transactionalism is strongly opposed to any mentalistic, "idealistic" framework for inquiry into knowings and knowns, the "realistic" alternative is also opposed. To affirm, as some epistemological realists do, that we in fact know some objects just as they are, is dogmatic and doubtful. Dewey and Bentley are among the few recent philosophers to take seriously some of the social science findings on human perception. Those findings make many philosophic views about observation and perception innocent indeed. The Ames experiments on perception are especially relevant here. Previous experiences of the perceiver, including his expectations, can play an important role in what is perceived. Bentley maintains that the Ames group's experiments on perception in distorted rooms, etc., reveal not only "illusion" in the ordinary sense, but "illusion so pronounced that doubt is cast on the apparent 'actualities' or 'realities' of ordinary visual report." He also says:

> ". . . perceptions as they come cannot be referred flatly to outer objects, nor to inner capacities as producers; and no more to the latter when neurologically postulated than when taken in the old slipshod form of the 'psychic.' "[23]

Much of the labored work in epistemology is bypassed, then, in favor of a scientific approach centering on what in fact can be, and is, found in inquiry. Such an approach is favored by many working behavioral scientists, of course, although it seems crude and inadequate to a great many philosophers. It may be mentioned that

---

[22]*Ibid.:* p. 56.

[23]For a convenient account of some of this work, see three papers with the general title, Psychology and scientific research, by H. Cantril, A. Ames, Jr., A. H. Hastorf and W. H. Ittelson: *Science, 110,* 1949. The quotations from Bentley are from Chapter 20 of his *Inquiry Into Inquiries*, Boston, Beacon Press, 1954, p. 352.

the supposedly naive scientists often work with views about human perception that are unusually complex compared to philosophic views on the same topic. One need only mention the frequency with which epistemologists rely on the unimpeachability and indubitableness of certain perceptual reports, to be assured of that point. In short, in their search for an ultimate ground for knowledge, or some certain starting point, or something fixed against all doubt, philosophers have all too often ignored the complexity and the uncertainty of those supposed fixities. Epistemologists raise doubts that in the context of ongoing inquiry seem pointless, and accept what in the context of inquiry seems highly doubtful.

7. CRITICISM OF TRANSACTIONALISM

Although a great many traditional philosophic and epistemological criticisms might be made of transactionalism, they will not be considered here. In later chapters, some of the objections to a scientific view of human behavior will be analyzed, so here it is appropriate to restrict discussion to criticisms coming from within a scientific framework.

A type of criticism that may be widespread has been raised by the anthropologist, Leslie White. He discusses a typical stock market transaction and maintains that scientific progress often results from concentrating on specific, manageable, abstracted aspects of a transaction, rather than on the whole process:

> "The scientist *never* grapples with *all* of the interrelated phenomena that confront him in a given situation. To do so would be to embrace the cosmos every time a sparrow falls. This is undesirable as well as impossible. The scientist must always abstract a certain segment of reality, a certain class of phenomena, from all others, and deal with it *as if* it existed by itself, independent on the rest."[24]

Even those sympathetic to the general transactionalist point of view may agree that sometimes the defenders of that view are so prone to emphasize the many items in the transactional field, and their relations, that inquiry never gets started. Rather than facilitating inquiry, then, it may be thought that inquiry is hindered by the emphasis on so many factors all at once.

---

[24]Leslie A. White: *The Science of Culture*, New York, Grove Press, 1949, p. 61.

Yet a more detailed analysis undermines at least some of the plausibility of such criticisms. In the first place, the attempt to inquire along self-actional and interactional lines often has produced no warranted assertions worth bothering about. The separation of presumed detachable elements, so much deplored by Dewey and Bentley, seems to be a widespread phenomenon in attempts to study human behavior. It is interesting to note that White's strong aversion to a mind-body dualism not only would elicit sympathy from Dewey and Bentley, but the very passage[25] in which White criticizes such a dualism might have been written by them.

Perhaps the issue is not so much the extent of the transactional "field" for any given inquiry, but rather a question of how much can be omitted without undermining successful inquiry. The specific examples given by Dewey, Bentley, and other transactionalists often are those in which significant scientific results were not forthcoming on the basis of self-actional or interactional theories. The question is not one of stating, in advance of inquiry, how much or how little should be included, but rather of including as much as is necessary to arrive at warranted assertions.

On many occasions the amount of control possible in an inquiry may be negatively correlated with the number of processes being considered. But at the same time, assumptions about those processes may have great significance for the results obtained. Let us consider an oversimplified example. Suppose some test purportedly measuring mechanical aptitude is given to many subjects, and all questions about the reliability and validity of the test are suppressed. This certainly simplifies the inquiry, and warranted assertions can be made as to the scores of the various subjects on the test. But presumably the test would be administered in order to find out how well given subjects are likely to perform mechanical tasks. If the test is a poor one, the administering of it may be futile.

Since, as already mentioned, it seems tempting for humans to assume as universal what in fact is highly localized, the emphasis on transactionalism may be of considerable help in predicting human behavior more accurately, rather than an unnecessary complication.

Other critics will see a vicious circularity in transactionalism. Not only traditional theories of knowledge, but many philosophies

[25]*Ibid.:* Chapter IV, Mind is minding.

of science, emphasize consistency of logical structure above other considerations. For such approaches, Dewey and Bentley may seem to compound all the confusions at once. Indeed, at a guess, a major reason some reviews of *Knowing and the Known* were unfavorable is the insistence of Dewey and Bentley that in one sense a circular approach is proper. For example, although they severely criticize others for introducing unobservable entities, Dewey and Bentley also emphasize the ease with which "firm" observations can go wrong. They choose certain postulates that stem from observation, yet use the postulates to increase efficiency of observation. If need be, the postulates are allowed to undergo modification as inquiry dictates. By refusing to start from any assumed indubitable base, they run counter to some prominent approaches today. Indeed, they say that although circularity "is regarded as a radical defect by non-transactional epistemological inquiries that undertake to organize 'independents' as 'reals,'" it is normal for their type of inquiry.[26]

In the present author's opinion, the kind of circularity advocated above amounts to no more than the kind of circularity found when man uses one tool to produce a better one. It is vicious only if viewed in a highly artificial context that ignores the developmental, process, side of the world. If knowers and knowns do transact, it seems prudent to recognize that fact rather than to deplore it or continue to erect epistemologies that seek to give an arbitrarily favored position to some one aspect of the transaction.

That the issue may have some point can be illustrated by reference to a recent article by Norwood R. Hanson. He argues at considerable length that the history of science "has *no* logical relevance whatever" to the philosophy of science, and is greatly concerned to avoid the "genetic fallacy." Hanson puts much emphasis on the philosopher's role in evaluating the arguments set forth by scientists, and holds that quite often the best argument at a particular time, given the data then available, is not the argument "that is ultimately correct." He maintains that this point "is of the utmost importance to any historian or philosopher of science," and says the discovery that "scientific advance and rigorous logic do not always walk arm in arm is an exciting disclosure."[27]

---

[26]Dewey and Bentley: *op. cit.*, p. 291.

[27]Norwood Russell Hanson: The irrelevance of history of science to the philosophy of science, *Journal of Philosophy*, LIX:581, 578-79, 1962.

The latter statement seems to illuminate Hanson's general theoretical outlook much more than it does scientific inquiry. Unless one were already committed to a view emphasizing logical consistency, it would hardly come as a surprise that rigorous logic and scientific advance are not always correlated. This, of course, is not to denigrate logical consistency, but only to point out that successful scientific inquiry is not the same thing as internal logical tightness. The widespread assumption that the two are more closely related than the facts warrant illustrates the danger of developing accounts of scientific method in separation from actual inquiry.

8. SOME ADVANTAGES OF TRANSACTIONALISM

If one looks at the formal definitions workers in various behavioral areas give for their fields, the results are sometimes discouraging. Imperialistic and aggrandizing tendencies are frequent; it is amazing how many disciplines study "all" human behavior without restriction. Indeed, if one did not already know which field was being defined, it would be almost impossible to guess from the definition.[28] Such evidence, however, probably deserves little weight. Presumably those offering such definitions are anxious to be inclusive enough to take in the work actually being done in their

---

[28]For example, anthropology has been taken as "the science of man and his works," and its subject matter has been said to include "all the phenomena of the social life of man without limitation of time and space." Sociology is said to deal with "the general characteristics of human groups in space and time," and has been taken as "a body of related generalizations about human social behavior arrived at by scientific methods." Economics has been said to deal with "man's purposive aiming at the attainment of ends chosen." History has been said to have as its object "the development of human societies in space and in time." Psychology has been described as the study of the "individual in interaction with his environment," and as "the systematic study, by any and all applicable and fruitful methods, of organisms in relation to their behavior, environmental relations, and experience." In order, the quotations are from: Ralph Linton, ed.: *The Science of Man in the World Crisis*, New York, Columbia University Press, 1945, p. 3; Franz Boas: Anthropology, *Encyclopaedia of the Social Sciences*, New York, Macmillan, 1930, Vol. II, p. 73; Stuart C. Dodd: *Systematic Social Science*, Lebanon, American University of Beirut, 1947, p. 2; G. A. Lundberg, C. C. Schrag and O. N. Larsen: *Sociology*, rev. ed., New York, Harper, 1958, pp. 6-7; Ludwig von Mises: *Human Action: A Treatise on Economics*, New Haven, Yale, 1949, p. 880; Henri Pirenne, quoted by Henri Berr and Lucien Febvre: History, *Encyclopaedia of the Social Sciences*, 1932, Vol. VII, p. 358; Walter Reitman: Psychology, in Bert F. Hoselitz, ed.: *A Reader's Guide to the Social Sciences*, Glencoe, Ill., Free Press 1959, p. 212; and *The Place of Psychology in an Ideal University*, Cambridge, Harvard University Press, 1947, p. 2.

field, and they may also want to be able to include work that some-
day may be done.

More significant evidence comes from the great increase in interdisciplinary efforts, team research, and the rise of new disciplines to
fill the gaps between existing ones. It seems clear that the conventional academic division of labor is neither coherent nor very helpful. The futility of trying to separate man's economic behavior
from his other behavior, for example, hardly needs documenting.
Some of the other divisions of effort also seem highly suspicious.
To mention one instance, some psychologists still formally describe
their field as concerning individual rather than social behavior.
But if social behavior were truly excluded from psychology,
the unemployment rate for psychologists would rise sharply. To
study human behavior as it occurs in ongoing transactions, then,
seems to offer more hope than to divide human behavior arbitrarily
into categories that apparently cannot be used effectively.

Emphasis on transactionalism may also lead to better experimental control in some situations. Illicit generalizations have sometimes been made from data because certain variables, assumed to be
irrelevant, turned out to be relevant. The work of Rosenthal and
others on experimental bias (cited in Ch. I of this book) illustrates
what is intended here. In addition, factors already referred to, such
as institutional, class, and cultural differences, may be of importance. For example, L. H. Levy and T. B. Orr analyzed both
the construct validity and the criterion validity of Rorschach tests
for a five-year period, and found significant relationships among the
researchers' institutional affiliations, the kind of validity study
made, and the estimation of the support given by the data to the
type of validity studied. (Researchers with academic affiliations, for
example, had favorable outcomes in 70% of their construct validity
studies, compared to only 50% of those conducted by nonacademic
researchers. Academic researchers found only 34% of the criterion
validity studies favorable, but nonacademicians found 59% favorable.)[29]

---

[29]L. H. Levy and T. B. Orr: The social psychology of Rorschach validity research,
Journal of Abnormal and Social Psychology, *58*, 1959.

Certain phenomena that seem to upset some people considerably also take on a less disturbing aspect when viewed transactionally. Some, for example, have argued that self-fulfilling or self-defeating prophecies show that human behavior is basically unlike the behavior of other portions of nature. Perhaps even more frequently urged is the view that a basic demarcation between the natural and social sciences flows from the fact that the prediction of human behavior may alter that behavior, whereas the prediction of say, an eclipse, does not alter the eclipse's behavior.

The human behavior in question does not seem surprising when viewed transactionally. Humans transact with each other in many ways, and obviously an enormous amount of human activity is responsive to the behavior of other humans. If warranted assertions can be developed that adequately describe those occasions in which self-fulfilling prophecies are like to occur, or those on which people behave so as to defeat a publicized prediction of their behavior, a scientific approach will have been preserved. Given certain conditions, one attempts to predict a sequence of human behavior. Included among those conditions may be behavior of the scientist, the published predictions of the behavior under study, etc. That a person may respond differently, once aware of certain behavior of the scientist, than he would have responded had he not been aware of that behavior, does not seem particularly upsetting, nor does it seem fatal to a scientific study of human behavior. Presumably in scientifically studying the behavior of any kind of object, it is necessary to identify and measure the factors influencing it.

Perhaps some commentators are excited about the phenomena just discussed because they implicitly or covertly regard the experimenter as existing in a different realm from the subject, or assume some "elements" are detachable when in fact they are not. (Indeed, from a transactional view it would be surprising to find that people *are not* influenced in some way after they learn of predictions about their behavior.)

9. CONCLUSION

The position advocated in this chapter is very close to, although not identical with, the transactionalism of Dewey, Bentley, and others. The position is advocated, however, only in a tentative and experimental spirit.

Dewey and Bentley are themselves very clear on this point. They take "postulate" in the sense of "a condition required for further operations," and say they want their postulations both to come from observations and be used to "increase efficiency of observation, never to restrain it."[30] In the same vein, a transactional approach as here advocated is taken as always open to re-examination. It is not held as the only useful approach, or as always the best method, nor is it said to be conclusively proved. It is supported as an approach that seems appropriate for many behavioral science inquiries, that helps to eliminate some of the difficulties of other approaches, and is tentative enough not to impede inquiry.

---

[30]Dewey and Bentley: *op. cit.*, p. 80.

4

PROBLEMS, TECHNIQUES, AND PRIORITIES
OF RESEARCH

1. INTRODUCTION

ALTHOUGH sociologists and psychologists have shown most interest in the complex of problems involved here, the problems are relevant to behavioral science in general. As is so often the case, the lines of dispute are far from neat and tidy. At times quite different problems are given the same label, and at other times very similar problems are discussed under different labels. The aim in this chapter is to focus on a core of related and complex issues, without attempting exhaustive coverage.

One recurring theme concerns the "burning issues" of the day. Some behavioral scientists have criticized their colleagues strongly for not concentrating on the crucial human problems of man in society. Robert S. Lynd, in his well-known book *Knowledge for What?*, is critical of the view that each scientist should "shape his bricks of data and place them modestly on the growing pile." This fails to work, he says, or does not work "fast enough to provide a social science corpus on which a floundering world can rely." Lynd also warns against the investigation of only those aspects of problems for which "good" (objective, statistical, etc.) methods are now available.[1]

Others have insisted that a carefully controlled natural science approach is of major importance; if that approach has had success in only relatively restricted areas, so be it. Kenneth W. Spence, for example, in answering the criticism that experimental psychologists have ignored pressing human problems in favor of simpler problems such as animal learning, says:

"Being guided by . . . purely scientific objectives, and not having any special interests, humanitarian, religious, social betterment or

---

[1] Robert S. Lynd: *Knowledge for What?*, Princeton, Princeton University Press, 1939, pp. 16-18.

otherwise, no particular area of human or animal behavior is seen
as more important than another [by the experimentalist]."[2]

Should behavioral scientists focus on those problems for which
scientific techniques are presently available, should they turn to
crucial human issues that existing scientific techniques are not
adequate to handle, should they work on both, or can any priorities
at all be set?

There are commentators who see the present situation as a polar-
ized one. On the one hand are those using excellent scientific
methods on almost trivial problems, and on the other are those
working on important problems, but not in a way that can be called
scientific. Dan L. Adler, for example, thinks that personality
studies illustrate this polarization. The experimentalists, he maintains, seem to have narrowed the breadth of their inquiries and
often are absorbed in "details and specious variables." The clin-
icians, he goes on, cannot be said to have forsaken scientific method,
mainly because they have never adopted it. Although their explanations have breadth, they lack adequate evidence.[3] C. Wright
Mills polemicized against the bifurcation in sociology between the
"grand theorists" and the "abstracted empiricists."[4]

Often, unfortunately, humans exhibit marked differences of
opinion as to what is significant, important, or interesting. It would
be too much to expect that scientists will always agree, for their
personal needs, training, the intellectual climate of their discipline,
etc., may influence what is regarded as important. Those hostile to
behavioral scientists may find most such scientific work "either
hopelessly vague or hopelessly banal," as we have seen.[5] And of
course work that initially seems trivial may turn out to have direct
effects that all of us, or nearly all, would regard as highly significant.
As A. J. Carlson says, the "failure of bacteria to survive in close

---

[2]Kenneth W. Spence: The empirical basis and theoretical structure of psychology,
*Philosophy of Science, 24:*103, 1957.

[3]Dan L. Adler: Some recent books on personality, *Psychological Bulletin, 51:*284, 1954.

[4]C. Wright Mills: *The Sociological Imagination,* New York, Oxford University Press,
1959.

[5]Raziel Abelson, review of A. I. Melden's *Free Action,* in *Philosophy and Phenomenological Research, XXIII:*616, 1963.

proximity to certain moulds looked trivial at first, but few informed people would label the discovery of that initial fact *trivial* today."[6]

2. THE "IMPORTANT PROBLEMS" POINT OF VIEW

A. H. Maslow has deplored the consequences, as he sees them, of the preoccupation of psychologists with means (techniques, instruments) rather than problems. He believes that undue emphasis on means has contributed to excessive stress on polish and elegance, and neglect of significance and creativeness; the elevation of technicians over discoverers; the overestimation of quantification for its own sake; the fitting of problems to techniques rather than evolving techniques suitable for important problems; the establishment of a pernicious hierarchical system of sciences; an undesirable compartmentalization of sciences; the emphasizing of differences rather than similarities between scientists and others such as poets, novelists, and philosophers; the establishment of a scientific orthodoxy that tends to inhibit new methods, excludes major problems and makes science conservative; and the neglect of values.[7]

Gordon Allport believes that many psychologists ignore the "existential richness of human life" because appropriate hard science methods are not available for dealing with that richness. The temptation to "emulate the established sciences" makes for concentration on relatively trivial problems. "Special aversion attaches to problems having to do with complex motives, high-level integration, with conscience, freedom, selfhood." He wants to see a "psychology of becoming" developed, and thinks we can find the outlines "by looking within ourselves; for it is knowledge of our own uniqueness that supplies the first, and probably the best, hints for acquiring orderly knowledge of others."[8]

Arnold M. Rose argues that in sociology the methodological issue of whether subject matter or method should be primary underlies a

---

[6]As quoted by George A. Lundberg: *Can Science Save Us?*, 2nd ed., New York, Longmans, Green, 1961, p. 50.

[7]A. H. Maslow: Problem-centering vs. means-centering in science, *Philosophy of Science, 13*, 1946. Reprinted with minor changes in A. H. Maslow: *Motivation and Personality*, New York, Harper, 1954.

[8]Gordon Allport: *Becoming: Basic Considerations for a Psychology of Personality*, New Haven, Yale University Press, 1955, pp. 11-12, p. 23.

great many other issues.[9] As he analyzes the controversy, the advocates of the primacy of subject matter believe that research topics are set either by theoretical developments within science or by value premises outside of science. The selection of a topic is extremely important, but the criteria for selection need not be scientific. The techniques used to investigate the topic should be adapted to the topic. Rose identifies himself with the advocates of subject matter primacy.

The proponents of method, he goes on, maintain there is *one* scientific method, but of course admit that many different techniques can be used in that method. They also hold, according to Rose, that research topics should be chosen that can be handled by the method. The supporters of the primacy of method accuse their opponents of being "philosophic" and of not understanding the need for scientific rigor.

Some of the complications and possible confusions of the general controversy are illustrated in other remarks by Rose. He proposes defining "science" as a "body of valid knowledge, where validity can be tested by making predictions from the knowledge that prove to have an accuracy that is beyond that which could be expected by chance alone."[10] He then suggests the primacy of method school holds that the "inductive, experimental method" is the only way of producing valid predictions. He contrasts the following methods with experimental method:

"... extrapolation of historical trends, structural analysis of functionally related components of a society or a personality, logical deduction from truisms resting on empirically verified assumptions, comparisons from history or ethnology, applications of generalizations arrived at by analytic induction through modification of hypotheses by successive tests with exceptional cases, application of generalizations arrived at by statistical measures of correlation or significance."[11]

Some who advocate the primacy of method, however, would not be willing at all to restrict themselves to "experiment" in the sense

---

[9]Arnold M. Rose: *Theory and Method in the Social Sciences*, Minneapolis, University of Minnesota Press, 1954, Ch. 14.
[10]*Ibid.:* p. 246.
[11]*Ibid.*

Rose gives that term. At least some of the contrasting methods mentioned by Rose would be acceptable to hard science supporters. Indeed, they frequently point out that in a well-developed science such as astronomy, strict experimentation is often impossible, and that comparative methods have important uses in, for example, the biological sciences.

In short, disagreements about the specification of hard science techniques are sometimes intermixed with disagreements about the relative priority of techniques and problems. The disagreements as to "science" seem partly semantic and partly technical. Rose, for example, argues that certain statistical techniques frequently used by sociologists cannot be regarded as equivalent to experimental control.[12] Hard science supporters are likely to insist that non-experimental inquiries can be controlled satisfactorily, sometimes to a degree equivalent to rigorous experimentation. Whether given statistical devices are in fact equivalent to experimentation is of course important, but separate from the larger question. Disagreements about the range of techniques admitted as properly scientific, and technical questions about the merits of specific techniques, then, may be involved in some discussions of the relative priority of problems and methods.

Some clinical psychologists have suggested that those focusing on methods do so because of their personality structure. Seymour Fisher and Rhoda Fisher, for example, see a relation between personal insecurity and attitudes toward methodology, and say that "many highly anxious individuals try to control and hide their anxiety by engaging in superformalistic and precise behavior."[13] Personality structure arguments have also been used to defend the other side of the controversy, as we shall see.

3. THE "HARD SCIENCE" POINT OF VIEW

Much of Spence's discussion of the issue seems typical of a prominent point of view. Spence agrees with the critics that his type of psychological research has concentrated on the "simpler" areas. He denies that this was done because of any aversion to more

---

[12]*Ibid.:* p. 247.

[13]Seymour Fisher and Rhoda Fisher: Relationship between personal insecurity and attitude toward psychological methodology, *The American Psychologist, 10:*539, 1955.

complex areas, but for strictly scientific reasons. The attainment of the type of knowledge found in the natural sciences requires "methods of observation that assure publicly verifiable concepts." But even more important, he says, "has been our estimate of the likelihood of successful accomplishment of our aim of discovering scientific laws about the phenomena." The simpler phenomena were chosen because progress seemed more likely than in the case of complex behavior. He adds that presumably what is discovered about the simpler behaviors will also be operative in more complex behaviors, probably interacting there with additional factors. In the long run, therefore, it may be more efficient to concentrate first on simpler phenomena.[14]

However, Spence goes on to say he should not be understood as advocating the neglect of the relatively complex aspects of personality. He thinks, as a matter of fact, that attempts to investigate those aspects scientifically have been reasonably successful, as in the areas of human adjustment, conflict and anxiety, complex motives, attitudes and interests, and problem solving and reasoning.[15]

Here another complication may be mentioned. Although many hard science supporters presumably would agree with what has here been summarized of Spence's views, they might also object to other aspects of his position. Spence was strongly influenced by logical empiricism, and in the article under discussion advocates a strict physicalistic position, being careful to say, however, that physicalistic procedures may not work in all areas. Although there are rough and ready differences between the hard science advocates as a group and their opponents, the differences among the members of each group are also important.

H. J. Eysenck has recently attempted to further the development of psychiatry on an experimental basis, and in so doing has been highly critical of many psychologists. He emphasizes the need for a firm foundation on which higher-order generalizations can be built:

> "In its present humble state, psychology can at best support on a factual basis certain low-order generalizations; to go beyond these is to court disaster. Such generalizations are the building stones for

---

[14]Spence: *op. cit.*, pp. 102-3.
[15]*Ibid.*: p. 103.

all future advance; hence the importance of deriving them from the facts in a proper quantified manner."[16]

Eysenck is convinced that what passes for science in the more complex areas of psychology is often pathetic. He describes his reaction after studying (during World War II) the textbooks on psychiatry and abnormal and clinical psychology:

> "The perusal of some fifty of these left me in a state of profound depression, as none of them contained any evidence of properly planned or executed experimental investigations, or even the realization of the necessity for such. Nor did I find that concise and consistent framing of theories and hypotheses which usually precedes experimental investigation; all was speculation and surmise, laced with references to 'clinical experience.' "[17]

His rejection of the scientific merit of Rorschach tests is equally uncompromising: "detailed investigation revealed all dross and no gold."[18]

As we saw in the previous section, some have suggested that personality factors incline certain researchers to emphasize highly controlled scientific method. We may now note that it has also been argued that personality factors incline some to accept confidently techniques that are very defective. For example, E. Lowell Kelly, in a discussion of clinical assessment, says: "the most widely (and confidently) used techniques are those for which there is little or no evidence of predictive validity." He goes on to suggest that those techniques must serve some other function, perhaps "to reduce threats of anxiety for persons confronted with the necessity of making significant decisions in the lives of individual clients."[19]

4. IMPORTANT PROBLEMS COMBINED WITH HARD SCIENCE TECHNIQUES

Some writers have urged an insistence on hard science techniques along with an immediate attack on some of the pressing problems

---

[16]H. J. Eysenck, ed.: *Handbook of Abnormal Psychology: An Experimental Approach*, New York, Basic Books, 1961, p. xiii.

[17]*Ibid.*: p. xiv.

[18]*Ibid.*: pp. xi, xii.

[19]E. Lowell Kelly: Theory and techniques of assessment, in Calvin Stone and Quinn McNemar, eds.: *Annual Review of Psychology*, 5:288, 1954, Stanford, Calif., Annual Reviews.

of men in society. The approach has much in common with the transactionalism of Dewey and Bentley, and has been vigorously advocated by the sociologist, George A. Lundberg. His views will be taken as fairly representative of this third general point of view.

Before discussing his position in detail, however, a further point should be made. The three-fold division of views in this chapter is intended as a convenient way of illustrating some of the emphases found in the literature, not as a hard and fast classification. Very few people, for example, would explicitly urge that the "burning" issues be ignored. At least some of the things Spence says are in agreement with Lundberg's point of view. And very few of the people discussed in Section 2 of this chapter would argue against the use of scientific techniques. However, taken as a matter of relative emphasis, the separation into three points of view has some utility.

Lundberg is well known, of course, for his advocacy over many years of a natural science *approach* to behavioral science problems. He has attempted to meet the usual arguments that human behavior is not amenable to scientific study, and is also insistent that scientific method not be restricted to the *techniques* used in the natural sciences.[20]

Lundberg objects to certain views about the relation of "values" to scientific work. He insists that the only proper value judgments made about *scientific data* are those relating to their relevance to the problem under study, the weight to be assigned to aspects of the data, and the interpretation to be made of what is observed. Such value judgments, of course, occur in the natural as well as the behavioral sciences. There is, however, nothing in scientific work *as such* that dictates the ends for which the results of the inquiry are to be used.[21] He argues that "the sole function" of scientific inquiry is to develop and publish "*systematically related and significant 'if . . . then' propositions which are demonstrably probable to a certain degree under given circumstances.*"[22] The scientist, *qua* scientist, does not determine the ends to which scientific findings are put. His business is to ascertain reliably the immediate and remote costs and consequences of

[20]Lundberg: *op. cit.*, especially Ch. II, Can science solve social problems?
[21]*Ibid.*: pp. 32-33.
[22]*Ibid.*: p. 35. (Italics in original.)

alternative courses of action. In the scientist's capacity as a citizen, he is of course free to advocate any course of action.

Yet Lundberg does not conclude from this that "anything goes," or that the line of action preferred by an individual is entirely arbitrary and subjective. He notes that some "fundamental aspirations and desires" of man have been "incorporated into his biology through ages of evolution" and validated through survival. Such desires and aspirations form a "sound foundation for an ethical system." But the difficulty has been, heretofore, that we have lacked reliable ways of finding out what man's experience has been and the actual costs and consequences of the lines of activity that have already been tried.[23]

Although in one sense of the phrase Lundberg urges a "value-free" science, he is strongly optimistic about the possible transformations in human life that could occur if a scientific attack is made on our problems. Science *can* save us. Yet he insists that comparatively speaking almost no fundamental research into human relations has occurred. Not only the financial costs of such research, but the costs in terms of giving up prescientific habits of thinking and analysis, would be great. On the other hand, we should not ignore the results that have already been achieved in a scientific study of human relations. Among other examples of such successes, he mentions some large scale predictions:

> "It remains a fact that social scientists predicted within a fraction of 1 per cent the actual voting behavior of sixty-eight million voters in the U.S.A. in the presidential election of 1960. . . . Nor are such results limited to voting behaviors. The late Professor Stouffer of Harvard predicted, also within a fraction of 1 per cent, the number of discharged soldiers after World War II who would take advantage of the educational privileges of the G.I. Bill of Rights."[24]

To summarize so far, Lundberg urges a broad yet hard science approach, sees some notable achievements to date in the solution of complex and important human problems, and holds that there are grounds for greater achievements in the future. But in view of the

[23]George A. Lundberg: Semantics and the value problem, *Social Forces*, 27:116, 1948. See also p. 113 of *Can Science Save Us?*.

[24]*Can Science Save Us?*, pp. 49-50.

magnitude of those problems, an enormous amount of scientific work remains to be done. What about those who say scientific methods are too slow in the face of our immediate vital needs? Lundberg says:

> "Well, we shall doubtless continue to suffer. Executives will continue to decide on the basis of guess and intuition and to mistake their own voices for the voice of the people or of God. The nations will doubtless continue to rage and the people to imagine vain things. . . . We shall probably become much sicker before we consent to take the only medicine which can help us."[25]

5. COMMENT ON THE ISSUES

Despite the fine things that can be said about scientists, they are subject to many typical human foibles. Although what we might prefer to see is the selection of significant problems and then the ingenious development of techniques suitable for their solution, doubtless many scientists, in many disciplines, will take whatever techniques are in good repute and use them on whatever materials come to hand.

One example may be mentioned in some detail. Leon H. Levy thought that in view of the present emphases in graduate study, psychologists might be more influenced by techniques than by problems. The Manifest Anxiety Scale (MAS) appeared in 1951, and the Children's Form of the Manifest Anxiety Scale (CMAS) appeared in 1956. Levy calculated the ratios of the number of entries under "anxiety" to the total number of entries in the indexes of *Psychological Abstracts* and *Child Development Abstracts*, for the years 1945 through 1958. For comparison, similar calculations were made for "drive" and "emotion" in *Psychological Abstracts*. Since the latter two notions are closely related to "anxiety," it was hypothesized that if psychologists had become more interested in that general type of problem, the increase of entries for all three terms should be proportional.

It was found that in the post-MAS period (1952 on), the increase in output on anxiety indexed in *Psychological Abstracts* was significant, and in the post-CMAS period the increase followed for

---

[25]*Ibid.:* p. 143.

entries in *Child Development Abstracts*. No concomitant rises were found for "emotion" and "drive." The author concludes that apparently research activity is controlled to a greater extent by techniques than by problems.[26]

Since presumably human ability for finding some use for existing techniques is likely to be greater than for developing new techniques, the results are not surprising. The fear of the problem-centered group that available techniques tend to dominate research may be justified. This is of great concern when there is reason to believe that the available techniques are very inadequate for the uses to which they are put.

Some writers champion the use of admittedly poor techniques until better ones become available. In discussing the situation in psychology, particularly the need for making critical decisions in the absence of warranted information, Walter R. Reitman says:

> "The interim solution is clear, if unsatisfactory. The work must be done, and certainly there are no people better qualified, by dint of their experience and training, to accomplish whatever we currently are capable of doing than those now engaged in this work. In the long run, as has been happening in medicine, intensive research will gradually improve the situation.[27]

Although no prohibition of using defective techniques if nothing better is available is urged by the present writer, the dangers are obvious. Only too frequently portions of the public may be misled if people taking the title of scientist rely on untested and admittedly poor devices. We should not allow ourselves to be persuaded that a defective or inadequate technique is better than it is, just because the need to solve some problem is humanly so important. It is not exceedingly difficult to get many people to assume that a given device, test, model, etc., has merit if it is used by prominent researchers and if major decisions are based upon it. What seems to be more difficult is to get people to remember that sometimes vari-

---

[26]Leon H. Levy: Anxiety and behavior scientists' behavior, *The American Psychologist*, *16*, 1961. The hostility in this article toward the work of B. F. Skinner and others is worthy of mention. The controversies in behavioral science can be as bitter as those in any other discipline.

[27]Walter R. Reitman: Psychology, in Bert F. Hoselitz, ed.: *A Reader's Guide to the Social Sciences*, Glencoe, Ill., Free Press, 1959, p. 238.

ous devices are used only because nothing better is at hand, and that very little confidence can be placed in the results of that use.

An interesting set of ideas is formulated by an econometrician, Eugene F. Elander, in a debate on mathematical models in the social sciences. His reply to an article critical of those models emphasizes that mathematical models offer great hope for accurate prediction in the future, even if existing models are frequently poor. Elander then goes on to criticize the authors of the earlier article for ignoring the role of models in formulating policy:

> "That econometric models . . . are useful in this way is beyond dispute—one need only look at the Netherlands, for instance, where an extensive policy-oriented model is used to guide government planners toward sound economic decisions."[28]

It is worth mentioning that Elander's use of "useful" is not clear here. He might mean only that in fact the models are widely employed. But this of course allows the possibility that their use is no better than prognostication based on the entrails of birds. If he intends to say that the models have provided successful predictions for the Netherlands government, it is odd that he cites the case after a discussion of the present methodological weakness of those models. It hardly seems safe to assume that a given device has scientific merit just because governmental officials use it.

A certain type of "realism" also seems important here. We may as well admit that highly skilled scientific practitioners sometimes make greater progress using relatively poor techniques than second raters do with well-developed techniques. The right man in the right place may get a glimpse of an important warranted assertion even with comparatively inadequate equipment, and future developments may give the desired degree of confirmation. Jean Piaget's work on the language, thinking, and moral standards of children seems to have stood up very well, even if his working conditions were far more primitive than those of many American researchers.[29]

---

[28]Eugene F. Elander: Correspondence on mathematical models, *Social Science, 37:* 249, 1962.

[29]For example, Jean Piaget: *The Language and Thought of the Child,* 2nd ed., New York, Harcourt, Brace, 1932; *The Child's Conception of the World,* Paterson, N. J., Littlefield, Adams, 1960; and *The Moral Judgment of the Child,* Glencoe, Ill., Free Press, 1948.

Perhaps it is basically misleading to focus too much attention on problems versus techniques. As nearly all parties to the controversy admit, there is a close relation between them. After all, a great many factors influence the alternative problems a given scientist or scientific team can choose from; to assume a practically unlimited range of choice may be quite incorrect. An unduly narrow view of what constitutes science, a conviction that certain behavior patterns are not amenable to scientific inquiry, and the inability to devise techniques that are at least minimally scientific, may all impede a resolution of major problems. Attacking basic problems with poor techniques, or trivial problems with good techniques, may produce a few helpful results, but surely what we need most is an attack on major problems with good techniques.

6. CONCLUSION

As observed earlier, as long as humans continue to exhibit the kind of diversity they do, we can expect some disagreement as to what the important issues of the day are. On the other hand, at least some problems are likely to seem major and basic to a large majority. For example, few are likely to deny that human survival constitutes a pressing problem. Possible damage through radiation, the inadequate diet of many members of the world's population contrasted to food surpluses in other places, and the much discussed population "explosion," are only a few obvious crises in human relations.

The tendency of mankind to rely on folk knowledge, "intuition," political leaders' expertise, or religious and ethical exhortation, to mention only some possibilities, poses a major difficulty. Without in any way overstating the already available results of scientific inquiry into the problems of men in society, the widespread conviction that those problems either are not amenable to scientific study or that short cut remedies can be substituted for that study, may be the chief hurdles to be overcome. Obviously great skill, ingenuity, and financial resources are required to arrive at the type of warranted assertions that offers hope for solving our problems.

In this context, perhaps the dominant reason optimism is in order about the possible achievements of science is the widespread acceptability of the results of well-controlled scientific inquiry. The notorious disagreements stemming from other modes of inquiry should hardly have to be mentioned here; yet many apparently need to be reminded constantly of the kind of agreement fostered by science. Without political, economic, or ideological coercion, the evidential weight of properly conducted scientific inquiry finds acceptability even in diverse political, economic, social, and cultural contexts. Perhaps the only real hope in the areas of discord that especially have plagued mankind through the centuries is the kind of warranted assertion produced by sound scientific work.

To avoid possible misunderstanding, it may be well to note that no magical dissolution of disagreement is here relied upon. Early in the history of natural science well-grounded assertions were sometimes ignored and the evidential weight of experiments disparaged. Perhaps some prejudices about human behavior are so ingrained that many will refuse to countenance the results of even the best work. After all, some people in our own time reject vaccinations, blood transfusions, operations, etc. Yet what mode of inquiry can even compare to the scientific in terms of acceptability across cultural, social, and ideological lines?

Earlier some dangers were noted even in the provisional use of crude and inadequate techniques and methods. The temptation to rely to an unreasonable degree on defective ways of solving problems seems to be a great one. But if degree of confidence is held roughly proportional to the weight of the evidence, some progress may be achieved by beginning with whatever minimally scientific techniques we have. Some usable results probably will be forthcoming, as well as ways of improving those techniques.

Some highly speculative theories, not in any sense scientifically tested, of course may be useful in important ways. Although it seems currently fashionable to denigrate Lucretius' theory of evolution, for example, it actually has many merits. Such theories, if subjected to scientific testing, might well on occasion produce significant results. But of course the difficulty has been that so often speculative theories have been accepted, and acted upon, not because of any empirical evidence, but rather because they were aesthetically pleasing, harmonized with dominant thought patterns of the time, satisfied individual psychological needs, etc.

The subject matter chosen for research, and the means chosen to pursue that research, are complex behaviors that are influenced by many factors. Throughout this book it is argued that in principle all aspects of human behavior can be investigated scientifically. Past successes of scientific method in the physical and biological fields suggest that the problems of men in society can be solved by the same method, if they can be solved at all.[30]

---

[30]For an account in considerable detail of some of the findings in the behavioral fields to date, see Bernard Berelson and Gary A. Steiner: *Human Behavior: An Inventory of Scientific Findings*, New York, Harcourt, Brace, and World, 1964.

5

CONTROVERSIES AS TO THE EXTENT SPECIFIC DISCIPLINES CAN BE SCIENTIFIC

1. GENERAL COMMENTS

VARIOUS factors make discussion of the general topic slippery and unsatisfactory in certain respects. Disputes as to the extent that history, for example, can be scientific are often grounded in disagreements about what constitutes scientific method. What on the surface seems to be a disagreement as to the applicability of scientific method in general may turn out to be disagreement about whether some specific technique is properly called scientific. On the other hand, arguments supposedly about the scientific propriety of specific techniques may be at bottom arguments about scientific method in general. The differing frames of reference used by participants in the controversies make it almost impossible, at times, to find out just what is being argued about.

Even so, to review some of the disputes as they occur in the behavioral literature is useful. For one thing, questions of concern to practicing scientists are not always those emphasized by philosophers of scientific method. For another, the disputes point up the need for greater clarity. The persistence of sloganizing is a prominent feature of some discussions.

Although the account given of scientific method in the early chapters of this monograph underlies the present chapter, other views of science often are held by participants in the debates here considered. Comparisons between various accounts of science are not explicitly made in the present context; the aim is to follow out the disputes as they occur.

Attention here is given to some of the older fields of inquiry: anthropology, economics, history, jurisprudence, political science, psychology, and sociology. This is done because work in such newer fields as game theory, decision theory, cybernetics, information theory, linguistics, and general systems theory is almost always at least nominally committed to scientific method. Some important and interesting questions arise as to the extent that work done under those labels is scientific; those questions are discussed in Chapter 2 and elsewhere. The present focus is on those areas in which some practitioners insist a nonscientific approach is called for, or that a scientific approach has grave limitations. In Chapter 6 some general issues concerning alleged differences between natural and behavioral sciences are considered.

Finally, as noted in appropriate places below, discussions about the merits and limitations of scientific method are more prominent in some of the older fields than in others. Often these disputes are related to the history of the discipline, the length of time professed scientific inquiries have been carried on in it, and the characteristic type of graduate education in that field. Although the intensity of the dispute sometimes seems to be correlated negatively with quantity of scientific output, it would be dangerous to assume any such general correlation. For example, disputes about the merits of a scientific approach are much more prominent in anthropology than in sociology, but it would be hazardous to conclude there was a corresponding differential in the number and significance of the warranted assertions discovered in the two fields.

2. ANTHROPOLOGY

According to A. L. Kroeber, the most important achievement in anthropology after the turn of the century was the development of a commonly held naturalistic approach. The values, customs, societies, languages and histories of men were taken as "being phenomena of nature to exactly the same degree as the biology of men." He adds that simple as the program was as an idea, operationally it was a difficult achievement, not easily won. For, as he points out, in a great many areas of human behavior, no matter what is said officially, "human activities are consistently set apart from nature."[1]

Kroeber's comments make a helpful point of departure for several of the things to be discussed. A dualism between man and

---

[1]A. L. Kroeber: *The Nature of Culture*, Chicago, University of Chicago, 1952, p. 143.

other aspects of nature is frequently a major obstacle to scientific inquiry into human behavior. Among workers in the behavioral disciplines the dualism is usually officially denied, yet implicitly it occurs frequently and colors much of the work and the controversies about the methodology underlying that work. Further, even though the adoption of the common naturalistic approach Kroeber talks about is widespread in American behavioral science, other questions arise as to the best methods for pursuing a naturalistic inquiry. Kroeber himself voiced many suspicions of viewing anthropology as a social science; he and others regarded the field as primarily culture history.

The impact of the American Historical School (Franz Boas, Clark Wissler, A. L. Kroeber, etc.) on cultural anthropology was a strong one. The school emphasized finding out what happened in the past, especially in preliterate times and nonliterate cultures. But discussions of the alleged differences between history and science seem murky and confused in anthropology, as well as in history. Anthropologists viewing their work as a kind of history seem to take the concentration on the *past*, the emphasis on specific, "unique" happenings, and the lack of strict experimentation, as major differentia between history and science.

Others skeptical of a scientific approach view anthropology in association with the humanities. Such things as understanding, empathy, and insight are thought more important than the usual scientific techniques. This approach has much in common with *verstehende* sociology and some developments in economic theory. It is not always clear whether such "understanding" is regarded as a technique superior to those of the sciences, or as a supplementary technique.

Finally, in some cases anthropology is thought of as an art form, in that an account of a culture is taken as a constructed work of art. Some commentators regard much of the work of Ruth Benedict and Margaret Mead as falling into this category.

Complicating the general controversies in anthropology is the fact that many anthropologists were trained in a manner characteristic of the humanities, and some writers evidently have little direct acquaintance with current scientific methodology. George P. Murdock goes so far as to say that among cultural anthropologists "only a handful are adequately grounded in scientific method," and that "anthropologists are extraordinarily naive in scientific matters."[2]

However, it should be kept in mind that very high standards are maintained in field work, and accurate description of the various facets of the cultures studied is much emphasized. The actual work done by anthropologists seems to have a much higher scientific status than some of the debates in the field would indicate.[3]

3. ECONOMICS

Strongly dominant in economics is the tendency to stress the development of tightly knit, consistent, and plausible theories. The deduction of consequences from those theories is emphasized, frequently without any parallel emphasis on the empirical testing of those consequences. The underlying hope is similar to that of philosophic rationalism. Some self-evident, certain, or otherwise allegedly unchallengeable postulates are held with great confidence, and the implications of those postulates are held with equal confidence.

Sometimes deductive approaches are relied upon because it is thought impossible to test economic theorems in the "real" world. So a "short-circuit" method is adopted, in which the theorems are checked subjectively against self-knowledge of behavior patterns. At other times, the conviction is that there is no need or point to such empirical testing.

Economists sometimes believe there is a universal "logical structure of the mind" and feel that the individual's understanding of his own mental states is all that is necessary to predict reliably the economic behavior of other people in similar situations. The crude mentalistic and culture-bound views of certain economists are

[2]George P. Murdock: Sociology and anthropology, in John Gillin, ed.: *For a Science of Social Man*, New York, Macmillan, 1954, pp. 26-27.

[3]For discussions of the controversies mentioned in this section, see: Oscar Lewis: Controls and experiments in field work, in A. L. Kroeber, ed.: *Anthropology Today: An Encyclopedic Inventory*, Chicago, University of Chicago Press, 1953; Robert Redfield: Relations of anthropology to the social sciences and to the humanities, *ibid.*; and C. W. M. Hart: Cultural anthropology and sociology, in Howard Becker and Alvin Boskoff, eds.: *Modern Sociological Theory*, New York, Dryden, 1957; Gene Weltfish: The perspective for fundamental research in anthropology, *Philosophy of Science, 23*, 1956; and Leslie A. White: *The Science of Culture*, New York, Grove Press, 1949, especially Ch. 14; and the Kroeber and Murdock references in notes 1 and 2.

almost incredible in view of the psychological, sociological, and anthropological findings that have been available for some time. However, insistence that we have some kind of direct introspective insight into our own purposeful behavior, that the results can be extrapolated to men in general, and thus that human action can be understood in terms of the operations of our own "mind," can be found in a prominent position in contemporary economic theory.[4]

A view with similarities to that just discussed, but far milder, insists that economic activity must be understood in terms of human motives, intentions, purposes, etc., and further holds that "hard science" inquiries either exclude such phenomena or cannot describe them adequately[5]. Such views may reject the universalistic assumptions described above, and may also doubt our ability to extrapolate from the motives of one person to other people. But much economic activity, it is maintained, must be understood in terms of motives, expectations, etc.

Other writers hostile to a natural science approach in economics put considerable emphasis on economics as an historical inquiry. They argue that economics is not (or at least not exclusively) concerned with finding possible uniformities, but rather with the description of particular historical facts. Supporters of this view may of course allow that economics has other functions than the historical, but they differentiate historical inquiry from scientific inquiry.[6]

Finally, some anti-scientific writers argue that at least some important segments of economics are better viewed as an art than as any kind of empirical or formal study.[7] This view may be associated with the notion that economics is a policy field, or that it is concerned with the *wise* use of scarce resources. The emphasis seems to be on the application of economic theories.

---

[4]For example, see Friedrich A. Hayek: *The Counter-Revolution of Science*, Glencoe, Ill., Free Press, 1952; Ludwig von Mises: *Human Action: A Treatise on Economics*, New Haven, Yale University Press, 1949, especially pp. 25-26; and Leland B. Yeager: Measurement as scientific method in economics, *American Journal of Economics and Sociology, 16*, 1957.

[5]For example, see George Katona's criticism of the report of the President's subcommittee on the behavioral sciences: Letter to the Editors, *Behavioral Science, 7*, 1962.

[6]For example, see Sidney Schoeffler: *The Failures of Economics: A Diagnostic Study*, Cambridge, Harvard University Press, 1955, p. 155.

[7]*Ibid.:* p. 156.

4. HISTORY

Several factors complicate the situation here. First, although the aim in this chapter is to emphasize the methodological views of practitioners, the relevant controversies in history seem to have been discussed primarily by philosophers. Second, competing and contrasting notions of what constitutes scientific method seem especially important in history; at times it is even difficult to ascertain what view of science is held. Third, in many disagreements one cannot tell whether the present (assumed) *practice* of historians is being discussed, or whether it is alleged that in principle historical inquiry cannot be scientific.

One often finds the view that history is concerned with the description of *unique* events, states of affairs, etc., and the sciences with *generic*, recurrent, repeatable events that can be predicted through general "laws."[8] As Adolf Grünbaum, Carey B. Joynt and Nicholas Rescher, and others, have pointed out, in a sense *every* specific natural occurrence is unique. Joynt and Rescher say:

"Galileo, rolling a ball down an inclined plane treated each roll as identical for it served his purposes so to do, just as an historian speaking of the Black Death could, if he wished, treat each unique death as identical in its contribution to a class of events called 'a plague.' "[9]

But many would maintain that even so, there is a basic difference between historical and scientific inquiries: science strives for the discovery of large scale warranted generalizations, and history is primarily concerned with particular facts. Here competing notions of what science is enter the controversy. If a view like that developed in Chapter 1 is held, the difference above is not particularly significant. The prediction (including retrodiction) of events is what is important, not the particular level of generalization.

---

[8]Some helpful accounts of the controversies here and some contrasting points of view are found in: Carey B. Joynt and Nicholas Rescher: The problem of uniqueness in history, *History and Theory*, *1*, 1961; Morris R. Cohen: *The Meaning of Human History*, LaSalle, Ill., Open Court, 1947, especially pp. 36-41; Edward H. Carr: *What Is History?*, New York, Knopf, 1961; Carl Hempel: The function of general laws in history, *Journal of Philosophy*, *39*, 1942; William Dray: *Laws and Explanation in History*, London, Oxford University Press, 1957; and Paul Oskar Kristeller: Some problems of historical knowledge, *Journal of Philosophy*, *LVIII*, 1961.

[9]Joynt and Rescher: *op. cit.*, p. 151. Also, Adolf Grünbaum: Causality and the science of human behavior, *American Scientist*, *40*, 1952.

Probably most commentators would agree that historians collect and examine data, formulate hypotheses, draw the consequences of those hypotheses, and test the consequences. The major issue then seems to be the type of method used to test the consequences, since the collection of data in historical research generally proceeds according to techniques that are here called scientific. If it is thought that history is somehow a special process, say an "irreducible activity of the human spirit,"[10] or is somehow *sui generis*,[11] then a great gulf does appear between science and history. But if scientific confirmation is taken as central, the gulf disappears.

Of major importance in this context are the varying interpretations historians give of what are supposedly the same events. The conflicting interpretations apparently flow from several factors: a) Sometimes the incompleteness of the available data allows for many interpretations; b) The ideological and other preferences of the historian may bias his results; and c) Use may not be made of already available warranted assertions from the various behavioral disciplines. Scientific inquiry seems to be the best device available for eliminating the influence of biases, and a better acquaintance with behavioral science findings on the part of historians may prove to be most helpful. But the sheer occurrence of diverse interpretations of data does not show that historical inquiry cannot be scientific.

Some commentators regard history as unscientific because "pure facts" are not obtainable. What "facts" the historian thinks he has found will depend upon chance, where and when he is looking, his methods, and the social influences upon him.[12] But this seems to be the case in all fields. What are commonly called facts issue from transactions between the observer and the field, as discussed in Chapter 3. To use traditional terminology, some facts are "harder" than others, and perhaps historians, for lack of relevant data, must often deal with relatively "soft" facts. But the transactional nature of the relation between so-called fact and the observer does not constitute a difference in principle between historical and scientific inquiries.

---

[10]Arthur Danto: On explanations in history, *Philosophy of Science*, 23:15, 1956.

[11]See, for example, Patrick Gardiner: *The Nature of Historical Explanation*, London, Oxford University Press, 1952, p. 32.

[12]See the first lecture in Carr: *op. cit.*

Moral judgment, too, has been thought to mark an important difference between historical and scientific research. Some believe a significant task of the historian is to pass moral judgment on the materials he discusses. But again, the situation need be no different than in other behavioral sciences. If an inquirer discovers warranted assertions, that is what is scientifically significant. He may go on to deplore, advocate, or remain neutral about what he has found. A sociologist who finds a correlation between illness rates and slums may deplore both illness and slums, but the adequacy of his findings does not depend on the moral judgments he makes.

In short, although it is clear that many historians do not proceed in a way that the present writer would call scientific, there seems nothing intrinsic in historical materials to make such an approach impossible. The view of science in the 1954 report of the Committee on Historiography of the Social Science Research Council is similar to the view set out in the present monograph, and there seems to be no reason why that approach cannot be applied with useful results.[13]

5. JURISPRUDENCE

Nonscientific approaches in jurisprudence are often accompanied by such confidence in their merit that not much is said in their defense. The long tradition of natural law theory and its recent resurgence help to illustrate the strength of nonscientific views.[14] The attraction of natural law theories seems to rest to a great extent on the hope of getting a basis for law that can be accepted with certainty.

This is not to say, of course, that more scientific views are lacking. The "legal realists" and the supporters of "sociological jurisprudence" have often advocated a scientific approach. Karl N. Llewellyn, for example, argued that the law is a body of data to be inquired into in the same general way physical scientists inquire into their data.[15] Recently Frederick Beutel has argued for an experi-

[13] *The Social Sciences in Historical Study: A Report of The Committee on Historiography*, Bulletin No. 64, New York, Social Science Research Council, 1954.

[14] See the issues of the journal, *Natural Law Forum*.

[15] Karl N. Llewellyn: Some realism about realism: responding to Dean Pound, *Harvard Law Review*, 44, 1931. Other helpful sources are: Edwin N. Garlan: *Legal Realism and Justice*, New York, Columbia University Press, 1941; Roscoe Pound: *Law Finding Through Experience and Reason*, Athens, Ga., University of Georgia Press, 1960; and Carl J. Friedrich: *The Philosophy of Law in Historical Perspective*, Chicago, University of Chicago Press, 1958.

mental jurisprudence that will bring both physical and behavioral science findings to bear on the problems of lawmaking and enforcement and will inquire into the effectiveness of statutes, as actually enforced, for accomplishing the purposes of the lawmakers.[16] Many writers on jurisprudence who are skeptical of their field ever becoming a science still urge the use of behavioral science findings.

Major doubts about the scientific possibilities of jurisprudence relate to the role of ought-judgments. Enormous energies in both traditional and contemporary jurisprudence are devoted to what laws ought to be made, how they ought to be enforced, etc. Roscoe Pound, for example, maintains that "what-ought-to-be" has first place in the social sciences, but no place in the physical sciences.[17]

Discussions of the relation of "ought" to "is" in jurisprudence concentrate so strongly on the modification and reform of existing legal processes that it is frequently difficult to discern exactly what is being advocated in terms of the methodology of legal inquiry. To some extent the issue rests on a confusion about a fairly simple distinction between warranted assertions in science and the application of those assertions.[18] The behavior patterns relating to legal and judicial processes can be studied in a strictly scientific fashion, and the warranted assertions resulting can then be applied, if people wish, to possible changes, reforms, and improvements. Predictions as to the probable consequences of a given reform also may be based on scientific inquiry.

The kinds of behavior involved in making, interpreting, and enforcing laws, the relations between the legal institutions and other forms of organized society, the relations between the legal processes and socialized preference systems, etc., all seem to be typical of the behavior that scientists have already successfully investigated. Doubtless many people will continue to try to develop better legal systems independently of scientific inquiry into the relevant be-

---

[16]Frederick Beutel: *Some Potentialities of Experimental Jurisprudence as a New Branch of Social Science*, Lincoln, University of Nebraska Press, 1957, p. 189.

[17]Roscoe Pound: *Contemporary Juristic Theory*, Claremont, Cal., Claremont Colleges, 1940, p. 36. Other interesting materials on the 'ought'-'is' relation in jurisprudence are contained in: Karl Llewellyn: *op. cit.*; Beutel: *op. cit.*, pp. 32-36; and George A. Lundberg: Conflicting orientation in law and national policy, in Richard W. Taylor, ed.: *Life, Language, Law: Essays in Honor of Arthur F. Bentley*, Yellow Springs, Ohio, Antioch Press, 1957.

[18]See Lundberg: *op. cit.*, p. 188.

havior, but such efforts do not show that a scientific approach is undesirable or impossible.

6. POLITICAL SCIENCE

Although the long standing association of political science with political philosophy, law, and history has tended to make a great deal of political science literature nonscientific, in recent years the rise of the "behavioralists" has centered attention on various methodological questions concerning the possible scientific status of the field.[19]

Some commentators believe that descriptive and prescriptive elements in traditional political science have been badly confused. The philosopher, George Sabine, for example, warns of confusing "states of facts, causal connections, formal implications, and the values or ends that a policy is designed to achieve."[20] On the other hand, Charles A. Beard once maintained that there was "no valid distinction between descriptive politics, political science, political theory, or political philosophy." A science of politics, he held, was neither possible nor desirable, for natural science methods are applicable in only a few instances, and not to the "fateful issues" of politics. The most that can be achieved is intelligence applied to political problems.[21]

A complicating factor here, as in other disciplines, is the divergence in views about what constitutes a scientific inquiry. Sometimes those hostile to science in politics seem to be referring merely to the fact that the specific techniques used in the natural sciences are hardly appropriate for political behavior. The discussion of scientific methodology on the part of political scientists seems much inferior, on the average, to that found in sociology and psychology. According to V. O. Key, Jr., as of 1958 the state of graduate instruction in the discipline was highly inadequate for the handling of research problems.[22]

[19]See Heinz Eulau, Samuel J. Eldersveld and Morris Janowitz, eds.: *Political Behavior: A Reader in Theory and Research*, Glencoe, Ill., Free Press, 1956, for a helpful account of the behavioralistic point of view.

[20]George Sabine: *A History of Political Theory*, rev. ed., New York, Holt, 1950, p. ix.

[21]Charles A. Beard: Political Science, in Wilson Gee, ed.: *Research in the Social Sciences*, New York, Macmillan, 1929, p. 286.

[22]V. O. Key, Jr.: The state of the discipline, *American Political Science Review, LII*, 1958.

The vigor of the recent behavioralists and their strong commitment to a scientific approach has resulted in counterattacks by those preferring a traditional orientation. In a recent volume devoted to a criticism of the scientific study of politics, Leo Strauss says it is doubtful that the new behavioral methods have produced anything not known just as well to the old political science (at its best), to intelligent political figures having a good knowledge of history, and even to "intelligent and educated journalists."[23]

Here again we get back to a classical philosophical problem: the grounds for reliable knowledge. Unless there is some prior agreement as to how we know we have reliable information, it is unlikely that we can get agreement as to the relative merits of scientific and nonscientific approaches. As argued throughout this monograph, a great merit of scientific inquiry is just that it fosters agreement where other methods of inquiry often do not, and agreement based on evidence rather than force.

Some writers, of course, are far less optimistic than Strauss about the significance of received results in political science. David Easton, for example, refers to the "disappointing results of a discipline already twenty-five hundred years old," and says a major reason for those disappointing results is "the constant reluctance in American political science to adopt and teach seriously the standards of . . . scientific method."[24]

It may well be that in a sense Strauss is correct, and that many of the views of older political scientists, politicians, and journalists will turn out to be warranted by scientific tests. But the obvious disagreements characterizing traditional discussions of political theory indicate the importance of a method leading to general agreement. The account given of the methods to be used by the behavioralists, and the problems they want to attack, are so similar to those already found in psychological and sociological research that there is not much doubt that the behavioralists' inquiries will continue to be successful.[25]

---

[23]Leo Strauss: An epilogue, in H. J. Storing, ed.: *Essays on the Scientific Study of Politics*, New York, Holt, Rinehart, and Winston, 1962, p. 312.

[24]David Easton: *The Political System: An Inquiry Into the State of Political Science*, New York, Knopf, 1953, pp. 3-4.

[25]See, for example, the comments by Eulau, Eldersveld, and Janowitz: *op. cit.*, pp. 3-4.

Perhaps the central reason some are suspicious of scientific methods is that the problems they are deeply interested in seem so complex and difficult that for a long time to come we may lack warranted assertions bearing on those problems. Hence it is tempting to turn to some other method that yields "answers," although those answers are not backed up by empirical confirmation.

7. PSYCHOLOGY

American psychologists are in the main strongly committed to scientific methods. There are some exceptions, of course, primarily in the social and clinical fields. For example, Thomas M. French, a psychoanalyst, says that sometimes the procedure followed is to "give free rein to the imagination," in hopes of seeing how the situation looks to the patient. The situation is then carefully examined "to test the intuitive impressions thus gained."[26] The testing of intuitive impressions against other subjective aspects of the situation may characterize a certain amount of psychological work, especially in the "looser" areas.

As in other behavioral fields, there are also those enamored of broad theories that are plausible and subjectively satisfying; often those theories may be accepted without any kind of serious or adequate empirical test. But, as is also characteristic of recent discussions in sociology, the major disagreements in psychology relevant to this chapter concern not the general method to be applied, but rather how scientific various techniques are, how useful various methodological assumptions are, etc. Thus controversies about behavioristic reductionism, the adequacy of experimental controls, the relation of theory and empirical testing, and whether allegedly empirically-based theories are actually so based, are much more frequently found than disputes as to whether or not some given psychological phenomena can be investigated scientifically.

This should not, of course, lead us to think that everything done under the official label of scientific work actually is scientific. Even those psychologists formally rejecting mentalistic terminology and notions sometimes fall into mentalism, and what passes for em-

---

[26]Thomas M. French: *The Integration of Behavior*, Chicago, University of Chicago Press, 1952, Vol. I, p. 29.

pirical testing is sometimes rather crude. Yet at its best, the relatively new science of psychology has produced a great many results, and one may speculate that successes to date are likely to help maintain the emphasis on scientific research.

Impatience with the frequent slowness of scientific progress and the keen desire to find answers to "burning issues," however, help to maintain nonscientific approaches. The recent appearance of existential psychology and humanistic psychology are illustrative of the dissatisfaction some have with conventional contemporary psychology.[27]

Rather than denying the relevance of a scientific approach into psychological behavior, then, those who tend to be suspicious of that approach are likely to hold that some areas of research do not lend themselves well to scientific inquiry, that some highly dubious techniques are scientific, or that inadequately tested theory can be relied upon.

8. SOCIOLOGY

American sociologists, too, show a strong adherence to a scientific framework for their investigations. Many of the disputes, as in psychology, concern the relation of the theoretician and the laboratorian, the merit of certain widely used techniques, and how well-confirmed given studies are. Some workers can be found, however, who advocate techniques that seem to be thought of as opposed, or partially opposed, to a fully scientific mode of inquiry. Those influenced by Max Weber's *verstehende* sociology emphasize the understanding of social behavior from the perspective of the behaver's subjective motivation.[28] Social action theorists frequently deplore the behaviorism of some psychologists, emphasize norms, values, and ends, and hold that introspection can be an indispensable source of scientific data.[29]

[27]For existentialistic psychology, see Rollo May, *et al.: Existence: A New Dimension in Psychiatry and Psychology*, New York, Basic Books, 1958. For humanistic psychology, see A. H. Maslow, ed.: *New Knowledge in Human Values*, New York, Harper, 1959, and the *Journal of Humanistic Psychology*.

[28]For a brief helpful account, see John C. McKinney: Methodology, procedures, and techniques in sociology, in Becker and Boskoff: *op. cit.*

[29]Preston Valien and Bonita Valien give a brief and useful description: General sociological theories of current reference, in Becker and Boskoff, *op. cit.*

Here again we are covering ground mentioned earlier. Those supporting scientific method put the emphasis not on the source of the data so much as on how hypotheses are tested, whether they lead to good predictions, etc. Introspective phenomena thus can have a place. The opponents of social action and *verstehende* sociology, however, are likely to say that what those schools call motives, purposes, etc., can easily be overemphasized, and that often what is desirable is an explanation of those motives rather than a reliance upon them as sufficient explanations.

Some sociologists put great emphasis on the deduction of consequences from highly general theories. Although his suggestion does not seem to have gained much support, Arnold M. Rose has discussed favorably the possibilities of a highly deductive method similar to that used by many economists. Certain "truisms" or "tautologies" would be heavily relied upon, and predictions then deduced from those truisms. Rose goes on to say:

> "It would thus seem possible that sociologists could develop a system of interconnected logical propositions from which important deductions and predictions could be derived that have as much validity as their original assumptions."[30]

One problem, of course, is that what are taken as truisms may turn out to be defective, or that what is introduced in addition to the tautologies, in order to make predictions of observed behavior, may be mistaken. The history of the problems associated with such approaches in economics and elsewhere points to the wisdom of being skeptical about its application to human behavior. In any event, if the deductions are subjected to the conventional empirical tests, then the method becomes part of scientific method as here understood. If not subjected to those tests, there seems to be no warrant to think of the procedure as scientific.

Some discussions of whether sociology is nomothetic or idiographic can still be found, although the issue does not seem to have the importance it once had. Nomothetic sciences are usually taken as those (such as the physical sciences) that search for warranted empirical generalizations; idiographic sciences are said to be concerned with particular historical occurrences.

[30]Arnold M. Rose: *Theory and Method in the Social Sciences*, Minneapolis, University of Minnesota Press, 1954, p. 342.

9. THE "POLICY" SCIENCES

Sometimes the fields much concerned with possible reform or with establishing guide lines for important decisions are called "policy" sciences.[31] For example, jurisprudence, political science, and economics have been taken as typical policy fields. Sometimes these so-called policy sciences are distinguished from "descriptive" sciences; it may be held that some sciences prescribe what ought to be done.

Others, of course, have argued for "value-free" inquiries, sometimes from very opposed points of view. George A. Lundberg, for example, is famous both for his support of a natural science approach in the behavioral sciences and for his insistence that the scientist, *qua* scientist, cannot dictate the ends to which his research should be put. Ludwig von Mises, who adopts a Kantian view of the mind and insists that awareness and analysis of our own purposeful behavior is the one scheme of interpretation available for understanding human behavior, maintains that economics is a theoretical science that should abstain from value judgments. "Science never tells a man how he should act; it merely shows how a man must act if he wants to attain definite ends."[32]

Difficulties are compounded, however, because "policy" is sometimes discussed, not in terms of the scientist, *qua* scientist, prescribing policy, but in terms of developing warranted assertions helpful for policy determination. Kenneth Boulding, for example, argues that policy studies are concerned with three things: what ends are wanted, how they may be gotten, and the nature of the group wanting the ends.[33] Harold Lasswell argues that policy sciences include the methods for studying policy processes, the results of such study, and the findings in those disciplines that make major contributions to "the intelligence needs of the time."[34] Both Boulding's and Lasswell's points seem compatible with the "value-

---

[31]See, for example, Ernest P. Hilgard and Daniel Lerner: The person: subject and object of science and policy, in Daniel Lerner and Harold D. Lasswell, eds.: *The Policy Sciences*, Stanford, Stanford University Press, 1951.

[32]Ludwig von Mises: *op. cit.*, p. 10.

[33]Kenneth E. Boulding: *Principles of Economic Policy*, Englewood Cliffs, N. J., Prentice-Hall, 1958, p. 1.

[34]Harold Lasswell: The policy orientation, in Lerner and Lasswell: *op. cit.*, p. 4.

free" point of view, for they apparently concern the scientific study of preferences rather than a statement of what those preferences ought to be.

A further problem arises if the policy sciences are thought of as fields directly relevant to the problems of, say, national policy. For then the line between policy and nonpolicy sciences would not only change through time, but the kind of separation between policy and descriptive sciences that is sometimes said to obtain would not make much sense. The development of physics to the point that thermonuclear warfare is possible certainly has a vital influence on national policy, and biological findings about radiation, fallout, etc., also affect that policy. Are we to say, then, that physics and biology are policy sciences? Many would say "yes," but then the two types of sciences would be differentiated merely in terms of their application, not in terms of the method used.

There probably is no harm in denominating as policy sciences those disciplines having a marked influence on policy at any given time, but one may well be suspicious of attempts to say that there is something special about the methods used to pursue such sciences. If, of course, it is maintained that certain types of scientific inquiry result in statements about the ends to which the science ought to be put, we might well have a significant way of differentiating types of science. That question returns to debates about the relation of "ought" to "is," the role of value judgments, etc., which will be discussed in the next section.

10. FURTHER COMMENTARY

The preceding sections were devoted primarily to a brief review of some major areas of controversy within behavioral disciplines about the extent to which those disciplines can be scientific. Any observer may misinterpret his data, but the aim, at least, was to illustrate current debates within the fields. Perhaps other topics than those listed will turn out to have greater significance than those here selected, and conceivably some of the current debates are misguided.

If we look at the fields in general, it appears that five different types of alleged limitation to a scientific approach (or ways of showing that those fields are not scientific) are often maintained. The five are: a) Empirical testing is unnecessary or only minimally relevant to the establishment of some results; b) Understanding or empathy is necessary in contrast to conventional scientific inquiry; c) Human behavior cannot be explained satisfactorily except in term of motives, purposes, goals, etc.; d) Not general statements, but accounts of specific occurrences are the goal of research; and e) The behavioral sciences are not, and cannot be, "value-free." Those five points will be discussed here; some related issues are taken up in the next chapter. It is interesting to note that the relative lack of strict experimentation is not stressed very often in the literature. Perhaps that lack is just taken for granted, or perhaps it reflects a widespread acceptance that strict experimentation is not a necessary part of scientific method.

a) Empirical Testing Is Unnecessary. As we have seen, there are a few workers who explicitly maintain that there is no need to test empirically at least some of the results of their investigations. There are many more workers who sometimes proceed as if they believed they had achieved results that could be accepted without testing.

The controversy is an ancient one. It will only be remarked here that it would be wonderfully convenient if we had some short cut way of getting warranted assertions about human behavior that would allow us to make accurate predictions. The problem is that the alleged direct routes to knowledge do not give us reliable, warranted information. The whole notion of science as here developed puts special emphasis on the testing of hypotheses. Any attempt to undermine or deemphasize that aspect of scientific method is a radical threat to scientific inquiry, as here conceived.

b) Understanding or Empathy. Obviously skill in empathizing with human groups can be a great aid in inquiry. An anthropologist who quicky grasps many aspects of the culture he is studying probably can formulate better hypotheses for testing, get his data more efficiently, be better protected against hasty generalization, etc., than a person finding the culture a great mystery. But there also can be dangers: the observer may project on the group under study what is true of some other group, or what he would like to think is the case. Many southern whites say they understand Negroes better than northern whites do, so at least one group of whites must be wrong in their "understanding." The question, of course, is how the understanding is tested. If taken as hypotheses to be tested rather than as direct insights into social facts that need no checking, there is no objection to using understanding.

In any event, a dichotomy between the cold, impartial scientific worker and the involved, sympathetic, nonscientific worker, is often superficially drawn. Some clinical psychologists have become worried about this issue. Carl Rogers, for example, sees a contrast between the scientist who takes the patient as an object to be manipulated in therapy, and the effective therapist who understands his patients. He also contrasts the objective understanding of people from the outside with an "existential" understanding from within.[35] But if a transactional view is adopted, the dualistic contrast does not make much sense in the first place, and the differences Rogers describes seem amenable in principle to scientific inquiry. Patients with presumably the same difficulty may react to different therapeutic approaches in markedly different ways; those differences can be described using the normal techniques of objective science. If the behavioral scientist is taken as trying to describe human behavior adequately, in specified contexts, there is no point in insisting he "manipulate," work solely from the "outside," etc.

c) **Explanations Must Be Made in Terms of Motives, Purposes, Etc.** From a transactional point of view, it seems likely that most explanations of human behavior will involve an account of motives. However, the proclivity of humans to be satisfied with verbalizations may lead some to give an unjustifiably privileged place to motive-accounts. As pointed out earlier, however, scientists often may be more concerned to describe and explain motives than they are to accept accounts of motives as adequate explanations. Suppose that in a given area, most Irish Catholic working class people vote Democratic in all elections. Suppose one such family votes Republican, and their purpose was to retaliate for some harm done

---

[35]Carl Rogers: Persons or science? A philosophical question, *The American Psychologist*, *10*, 1955. Also, Carl Rogers: Two divergent trends, in May: *op. cit.*

them by the local Democratic organization. This "explanation" would seem to tell us very little about the type of human behavior in question. As long as the family is motivated by strong hatred of the organization, we might say, they will vote Republican. But that comes close to being a tautology. A fuller exploration of how and why such motives develop, what might override them, and how they are related to other behavior, would probably give a better basis for prediction of the behavior involved.

d) Information about Specific Occurrences Is Wanted, Rather than Generalizations. To some extent discussions centering on the specificity of behavioral research seem to confuse the discovery of warranted assertions about human behavior with the application of those assertions to given instances. A somewhat parallel situation in physics and engineeering may be relevant. The warranted generalizations discovered about the field of mechanics have a very wide range, but the engineeer making use of those generalizations may properly be concerned about the stresses and strains in one particular piece of steel to be used in construction.

There is no need here to postulate some radical difference between "pure" and "applied" sciences; both the physicist and the engineer can use a fully scientific method as here understood. So too, at some given time, a relatively specific behavior may be of great national concern; for example, the possibility of strife in a basic industry at a critical historical moment. But if relevant warranted assertions about behavior patterns are available, we have a powerful tool for predicting, controlling, understanding and explaining such behavior.

This is not to deny that history as a discipline and the historical aspects of other disciplines are often primarily concerned with ascertaining as accurately as possible what happened in a given spatio-temporal context. There is a parallel here to what happens in the other aspects of science; that is, to have the best possible control over the data. Both the data and generalizations about the data are important.

Historical researchers use generalizations about human behavior to collect their data, interpret it, and predict what further data may be available and under what circumstances. They also may formulate generalizations; for example, about characteristic patterns of colonialism under a certain set of circumstances. Even so-called "brute facts" are interpreted by observers, and the notorious differences that sometimes occur as to what the facts are again support a transactional interpretation.

In short, those inquiries directed toward the description and explanation of specific occurrences do involve data collection and generalizations about the data, just as "nomothetic" inquiries do. The difference is one of emphasis, then, rather than a basic difference between the physical and the behavioral sciences.

e) Behavioral Sciences Cannot Be "Value-free." The variety of ways in which "ought" is used in these discussions is a source of considerable difficulty. Suppose we begin with a view often found, that scientific inquiry concerns the probable consequences of a variety of possible courses of action. Reliable information about the alternatives is discovered by scientists, and then the decision makers act on that information. Such an account of the situation is useful and sensible, for intelligent decisions about what ought to be done are obviously facilitated by an adequate description of the probable consequences.

However, the literature sometimes gives a peculiar status to the wants, "values," or preferences of people who make the relevant decisions. Those wants are sometimes taken as primordial, sacro-sanct phenomena that just occur, with science helping to supply the means to those ends. But surely there seems to be sufficient evidence to show that what we want, value, prefer, etc., is highly socialized. Scientific inquiry can be helpful in describing how wants develop under certain circumstances. Our preferences among preferences also are investigable scientifically.

Perhaps most participants in the controversy agree that the warranted assertions resulting from scientific inquiry do not include statements on the order of "You ought (absolutely) to do X." Rather, such inquiry issues in statements of the order "You ought to do X, if you want Y." The vexing philosophical disputes about hypothetical and categorical imperatives seem to have carried over into scientific contexts with no increase of clarity. But if the "Y" just referred to is taken as subject to scientific scrutiny, and if the probable consequences of achieving it as compared to other alternatives are considered, there is no neat and tidy limit to scientific inquiry, as sometimes imagined. Reliable information about human behavior, in the form of "if—then" statements, can move very far into the alleged value areas. Of course, if it is assumed that some things ought to be done entirely independently of consequences, then science is excluded from a study of those obligations. In such a case, however, it would seem hazardous to assert that any science (including the "policy" sciences) could be of much help.

Often debates on this general question are extremely murky. Irving L. Horowitz, for example, in an interesting article attacking "value-free" sociology and sociological empiricism, makes some useful points about the possible ideological uses of that type of sociology and the way it has become institutionalized in this country. He goes on to urge that sociologists should have much more influence on policy decisions than they now have, and takes as one reason for their relative lack of influence the rise of "value-free" sociology.[36] His *bête noire* in this respect is George A. Lundberg. But here Horowitz's argument becomes confusing, for probably no sociologist has been more optimistic than Lundberg about the ability of science to "save" us, and about warranted scientific assertions concerning human behavior being of the utmost significance for so-called policy decisions.[37]

11. CONCLUSION

Strong currents in many disciplines can be found that argue against a fully scientific treatment of the problems of that discipline. The lines of dispute, the structure of the positions involved, and even the relevance of much of what is said, are quite often unclear. Perhaps the overriding complication is the diversity of notions as to how scientific method is best specified. Once some particular way of using the term is adopted, much else follows logically. Frequently disagreements concern different views as to what constitutes science, not substantive issues within the disciplines. The assumption that the parties to the controversy share at least the same general notion of scientific method, when apparently they do not, helps to make many of the discussions highly unsatisfactory.

---

[36]Irving Louis Horowitz: Establishment sociology: the value of being value-free, *Inquiry*, 6, 1963.

[37]For a discussion of Lundberg's views, see Ch. IV, Section 4.

6

ALLEGED DIFFERENCES BETWEEN PHYSICAL AND BEHAVIORAL INQUIRIES

1. GENERAL COMMENTS

CERTAIN themes in this chapter, the preceding one, and the following one overlap. Separating the chapters as is here done is somewhat arbitrary, but is also convenient, especially for calling attention to the emotional and intellectual context in which the discussions occur.

The alleged methodological differences are here discussed in terms of *physical* and *behavioral* sciences. In the literature contrasts are often made between the natural and the social sciences, or between the natural sciences and social studies, or between the exact and inexact fields. On some occasions such terminological differences may be related significantly to the argument, but for present purposes there seems to be no harm in discussing the supposed differences as holding between physical and behavioral inquiries.

As Robert Brown points out, most philosophy of science literature falls into two classifications: that produced by philosophers for other philosophers, and that written by practicing scientists for other scientists. The failure of each set of materials to have much impact on the other is a notable aspect of the literature.[1] The emphasis in this chapter is on the views of philosophers.

Another complication is that widely varying frames of reference are found. Opinions about Quentin Gibson's recent study on the logic of social inquiry will illustrate the point. Gibson argues that natural science procedures are applicable to the study of social phenomena, but also that the subject matter of social inquiries results in "logical peculiarities" compared to natural science in-

---

[1] Robert Brown: *Explanation in Social Science*, Chicago, Aldine, 1963, p. 1.

vestigations.[2] Those steeped in the views generally advocated by American psychologists and sociologists are likely to criticize Gibson for overemphasizing the "logical peculiarities," and for admitting mentalistic procedures. They think Gibson does not move nearly far enough in the "hard science" direction. On the other hand, A. M. MacIver takes Gibson's book as "a work of religious apologetic, the religion being 'Scientism.' "[3]

Much rhetoric also stems from competing views as to what is characteristic, or should be characteristic, of behavioral inquiry. Within those disciplines some work is highly theoretical, some very empirical; some is consciously "hard science," while some is impressionistic, introspective, and intuitive; etc. Observers and critics thus may have in mind very different processes when they discuss behavioral inquiry. Brown devotes much of his book to an account and analysis of various explanations actually put forth by scientists. Some would find him too lenient, for he accepts as explanations what they would exclude as nonscientific, but others would find him too narrow and would want even "looser" explanations admitted. An observer, then, may make a distinction that correctly reflects a difference between physical science and *some* behavioral inquiries; those who deny what the observer in question maintains may have in mind very different procedures of inquiry. In short, sometimes those accepting a basic methodological distinction between physical and behavioral research take as relatively fixed features of behavioral investigation just what others regard as improper features of that investigation.

A good argument against those who maintain there is a basic distinction between the two modes of inquiry would be to point to behavioral inquiry results comparable to those obtained in the physical sciences. Since such behavioral results are not available, or available in minute quantity only, the discussion often shifts to possible future developments. Such a move may arouse the scorn of those opposing a "hard science" approach. MacIver, for ex-

---

[2] Quentin Gibson: *The Logic of Social Enquiry*, London, Routledge & Kegan Paul, 1960, p. 2.

[3] A. M. MacIver, review of Gibson's *The Logic of Social Enquiry* in *Mind*, LXXI: 271, 1962. The extensive commentary in this chapter on a brief review may seem unusual; it is done because MacIver's point of view is quite extreme, clearly presented, and illustrative of some current trends.

ample, objects that Gibson does not try to justify scientific inquiry in social studies by pointing to successes in the use of that method: "It is enough for him, as for so many religious apologists, to argue that what he accepts on faith has not been demonstratively proved impossible."[4]

Admittedly the exchange of arguments about possible future developments or about what can or cannot be imagined, is often frustrating and unsatisfying. To mention one illustration, some have maintained that free-will (in various senses of that phrase) makes it impossible to apply scientific method to human behavior.[5] Their opponents often fall back on replying that it is difficult to imagine how free-will could be demonstrated. Michael Scriven, for example, says he can see no way one "could establish the claim that human behavior is in principle undetermined and, hence, distinguish its study from that of the presumably determined inanimate world."[6]

Understandably, then, scientists may lose patience with controversies that run along the lines of X saying that you can never show all behavior is determined and Y saying that you can never show that at least some behavior is undetermined. The reaction of George Lundberg may be typical:

> "What about God and what about free will in a scientific world? Fortunately, we can answer this question satisfactorily, for all practical scientific purposes . . . That is . . . you may hold whatever views you like regarding both God and free will. All I need to point out and establish for scientific purposes is the great regularity and predictability with which men *will* things. I can predict the will and choices of men by exactly the same techniques I use to predict other natural phenomena. The same may be said about God. He is clearly a being with remarkably and demonstrably regular habits."[7]

---

[4]*Ibid.*

[5]See Felix Kaufmann: *Methodology of the Social Sciences*, New York, Oxford University Press, 1944, Ch. XIII, for an account of many senses of "free-will" and their methodological implications.

[6]Michael Scriven: A possible distinction between traditional scientific disciplines and the study of human behavior, in Herbert Feigl and Michael Scriven, eds.: *Minnesota Studies in the Philosophy of Science*, Minneapolis, University of Minnesota Press, 1956, Vol. 1, p. 331.

[7]George A. Lundberg: *Can Science Save Us?*, 2nd ed., New York, Longmans, Green, 1961, p. 107.

Yet in one respect there seems to be little choice about discussing what might or might not be done in the future. Although there are relatively few today who deny the possibility of physical science, there are those who deny the possibility of behavioral science. If it is granted that as yet there has been very little achieved in basic research into human behavior, clearing the way for such inquiry is helped by answering arguments that purport to show such research is either impossible or bound to be insignificant. This brings us to the first supposed line of differentiation between the two modes of inquiry.

2. HARD SCIENCE METHODS IN BEHAVIORAL FIELDS PRODUCE TRIVIAL RESULTS

As noted earlier, some critics think the application of scientific methods to human behavior yields only trivial, banal, and insignificant results. Undeniably behavioral research, at its worst, has produced much that is trivial by almost anyone's standards. Scanning the literature reveals a multitude of horrible examples. But whether or not the proportion of trivial materials is higher than in other disciplines is quite another matter. Browsing through philosophy journals for the past fifty years, for example, is not likely to leave one with the impression that most of the materials finding their way into print have lasting significance. The way research is institutionalized is also relevant. When enormous emphasis is placed on publication *per se*, when ambitious young scholars must tread carefully until they get tenure, etc., one may expect that much of the output, although publishable by conventional standards, will have no other merit.

To make any headway, then, we need to ask: "Trivial compared to what?" Sometimes scientific inquiry has been regarded as trivial compared to what poets, journalists, or other seers have achieved. The difficulty here concerns what standard of comparison we could appropriately use. Doubtless journalists have predicted election results, on occasion, better than some of the scientific polls. But how frequently, and with what consistency? One suspects that often the accusations of triviality are directed not so much to scientific inquiry into human affairs as to scientific inquiry in any field.

Romantics have long deplored science, and some still yearn for the kind of answer to "why" questions that scientists cannot give. It is interesting to note in this context that MacIver says "even if it is true that in physics we have to be content with empirical generalizations, the reason of that could be that we are not ourselves atoms or electrons, but in the 'social sciences' we might hope for something more, because we *are* human beings."[8]

Some maintain that scientific method produces trivial results compared to some other nonscientific method available to people in general. MacIver very succinctly and emphatically takes such a position. Science has as its purpose the prediction and control (in favorable circumstances) of events, he says, but a different purpose underlies nonscientific studies of human behavior. What is called "putting ourselves in another man's position" is not done to predict what the other man will do; however, after that person has acted "we do sometimes seem to understand *why* he did it." MacIver emphasizes that although we are not always wrong, it is "very easy" to be mistaken, and yet "there is no other way in which this understanding can be had."

Further, such understanding of behavior can be "really valuable." He gives as an example the case of labor unrest on the docks. The Minister of Labor, MacIver holds, does *not* want what a scientist could tell him of "laws" describing such behavior. The Minister would like to know "just what it is that these men really want, which might be something which they could quite easily be given, which would satisfy them."[9]

Surely, however, this involves prediction and control in just the sense scientific inquirers use those terms. Relevant "if—then" warranted statements could be most helpful to the Minister. If behavioral scientists could say with a high degree of accuracy what specific circumstances were likely to lead to particular kinds of labor unrest, and what would alleviate that unrest once it was engendered, wouldn't the Minister have exactly what he needed?

Indeed, one suspects that many past bungles in policy have resulted from an attempt to apply something along the lines that

---

[8]MacIver: *op. cit.*, p. 272.
[9]*Ibid.*: p. 271.

MacIver suggests. "Let them eat cake" illustrates one attempt of a person to put herself in others' shoes. The quip that one should not do unto others as ye would have them do unto you, because their tastes may be different, has its point. Governmental officials coming from very different sociocultural backgrounds than the people whose behavior they are trying to understand may project very mistaken attitudes on the other people. (MacIver, of course, insists that the attempt to understand may fail.) But again, do we not already have considerable useful empirical data bearing on just that topic? Class and cultural differences, for example, have been explored by scientific means. A good case can be made that both successes and failures in understanding others can be accounted for scientifically.

With some semblance of sense, the accusation of triviality can be turned around, and "inner" explanations dismissed as of little significance. When R. H. Lowie argues that in ancient Polynesia no sizable population was ever brought under a common head, "owing to the separatism of the natives," we may wonder whether anything at all has been explained.[10] To say that the Polynesians were separatists is to recognize an ongoing process; it does not give us much help in explaining it.

Conceivably (although I doubt it) the results of "understanding" have been less trivial than the results of existing behavioral science inquiries. But to say that such understanding is superior in principle to what could be done if the relevant "laws" of human behavior were available seems perverse and dogmatic.

3. COMPLEXITY OF HUMAN BEHAVIOR

Many workers in behavioral fields explain away their relative lack of success to date by invoking the complexity of the phenomena they study compared to the simplicity of physical phenomena. Michael Scriven has developed this point of view in a fairly elaborate way. He sees no reason for denying that "precise explanations and predictions are available or possible in the study of some behavioral phenomena," but thinks the difference between physical

---

[10]Robert H. Lowie: *An Introduction to Cultural Anthropology*, 2nd ed., New York, Farrar & Rinehart, 1940, p. 293.

and behavioral inquiries is "partly due to the relatively greater complexity of the *simplest phenomena we are concerned to account for* in a behavior theory." Behavioral scientists often "have to look for higher-order theories in order to get a lead on the variables to isolate for sound generalizations"; they have to run before they can walk. Although the same difficulty also occurs in other disciplines, Scriven thinks it is more common in the study of human behavior.

One result, according to Scriven, is that practical problems of prediction and explanation are more likely to be insoluble in behavioral than in physical inquiry. He expresses doubts that "simple laws" will be discovered comparable to those found in physics, and singles out as a major factor "the multiplicity of critical variables *in the simplest interesting cases.*"[11]

In strong contrast is the view of the anthropologist, Leslie White. After noting the tendency of many to blame complexity for their problems, he says:

> "They seldom explain what they mean by 'complexity,' and more rarely do they attempt to prove that complexity of phenomena must mean meagerness of scientific achievement. They merely assume, in the first place, that everyone knows what is meant by complexity, and, in the second place, they assume without argument that complexity means difficulty."[12]

White argues that social phenomena are no more complex than physical or physiological phenomena in the sense of "difficult to treat scientifically." The invocation of complexity is an attempt, albeit unconscious, to conceal helplessness. He holds that physicists know what their problems are and how to approach them, but behavioral scientists usually do not. The major reason, he suggests, is that both scientific technique and point of view have been developing for centuries in the physical areas, but are very new in the behavioral realm.

He also argues:

> ". . . we probably know more about stock markets than we do about gravitation. A war between two nations . . . is no more complex than the rusting of iron or the freezing of water. As a matter

---

[11]Scriven: *op. cit.*, pp. 331-36.
[12]Leslie A. White: *The Science of Culture*, New York, Grove Press, 1949, pp. 61-62.

of fact, it may be simpler than the formation of ice or a snowflake
. . . We understand symbol behavior (e.g., articulate speech) much
better on the psychological level than upon the lower level of
neurology. We know more about the psychology of jealousy than
its physiology. We understand the physiology of intoxication better
than its chemistry, and the chemistry of the glands better than
their physics. . . . One might well argue that as we approach 'ultimate reality' in physics the complexity of phenomena increases
and the difficulties of scientific explanation become greater."[13]

At least in part the disagreement between Scriven and White may
result from their differing general orientations. White is interested
in discovering regularities in human behavior; he seems relatively
uninterested in modeling statements about those regularities along
the lines of the "laws" of physics. Scriven, as is more typical of
philosophers, is extremely concerned about the logic of scientific
inquiry, and to some extent he seems to take physics (or certain
aspects of it) as the desirable model for behavioral science.

Although using the language of simplicity-complexity can be
tempting, often that language does not seem clear. Obviously some
transactional processes have more aspects that need to be differentiated than do others, or to use more traditional terminology, the
number of variables in some phenomena is much greater than in
others. But as Scriven notes, there is no absolute distinction between
physical and behavioral inquiries; some aspects of physics are
equally "complex." Possibly Scriven is right, and on the whole the
behavioral sciences have to deal with more complex phenomena
than other scientific fields. But we run the danger here of *a priorism*,
for in the future "simple laws" of human behavior may be discovered.
White emphasizes an important notion when he points out, in
effect, that the hold of traditional nonscientific modes of thought
and inquiry is so strong that often we don't know what questions to
ask or what would be appropriate means of solving them. Further,
physical phenomena that now seem simple probably struck the
original investigators as bafflingly complex. With a large body of
warranted assertions to go on, the complex may turn out to be
simple.

---

[13]*Ibid.:* pp. 62-63.

The literature on "laws" is enormous, and there will be no attempt here to assess it. But sometimes too much grandeur is attributed to physical "laws." After all, a great many assertions styled as "laws" are only approximations, holding in relatively restricted ranges. As Scriven emphasizes in another article, the main feature of "laws" is their inaccuracy.[14] Mario Bunge, with an interest in taking account of the sciences of man, suggests as a liberal criterion of "law":

> "A proposition is a law statement if and only if it is general in some respect (i.e. does not refer to unique objects), has been empirically corroborated in some domain in a satisfactory way (for the time being), and belongs to some theory (whether adult or embryonic)."[15]

Without entering into the merits of his criterion, it may be noted that the question as to what kind of "laws" may be expected in behavioral research is much dependent on how one understands that term and views its relation to controlled observation and experimentation.

Here again we return to the question of how scientific method is construed. Conflicting views of what constitutes that method may result in differing notions of the extent to which behavioral investigations can be scientific. So stated, the point may seem too trivial to mention, but frequently discussions of the general issue proceed as if all participants shared a particular view of science, or else the possibility of alternative views is not considered at all. One suspects the reason so many practitioners of behavioral science are convinced a scientific approach is possible and worthwhile is just that they do not take as narrow a view of scientific procedures as do many of their critics.

4. EXPLANATION, DESCRIPTION, AND PREDICTION

Sometimes it is alleged that behavioral research gives us mere description only, sometimes that behavioral research fails to pro-

---

[14]Michael Scriven: The key property of physical laws—inaccuracy, in Herbert Feigl and Grover Maxwell, eds.: *Current Issues in the Philosophy of Science*, New York, Holt, Rinehart & Winston, 1961.

[15]Mario Bunge: *The Myth of Simplicitv*, Englewood Cliffs, N. J., Prentice-Hall, 1963, p. 178.

duce satisfactory explanations, and sometimes that predictive ability based on well-confirmed generalizations does not yield "proper" explanations. In recent years quite a body of literature has developed as to whether or not explanation and description have symmetrical logical structures. The theme of a basic distinction between inquiry into nature and inquiry into human activity runs through many discussions of these issues.

The account given by Carl Hempel and Paul Oppenheim seems to describe the general situation well:

> "To explain the phenomena in the world of our experience, to answer the question 'why?' rather than only the question 'what?', is one of the foremost objectives of all rational inquiry; and especially, scientific research in its various branches strives to go beyond a mere description of its subject matter by providing an explanation of the phenomena it investigates. While there is rather general agreement about this chief objective of science, there exists considerable difference of opinion as to the function and the essential characteristics of scientific explanation."[16]

a) Description and Explanation. Brown seems to have answered satisfactorily those critics who maintain that mere description, and not explanation, is all the behavioral sciences offer. He considers a great many passages from the writings of scientists, and shows that what reasonably are called explanations are normally involved.[17] As we shall see, however, some critics may not accept the sense of "explanation" Brown uses.

As is generally recognized, sciences other than the behavioral contain so-called mere descriptions; the issue is whether or not the sciences of man can also yield good explanations. It seems to me that frequently far too facile a distinction is made between a mere description and something else. Of course a catalogue of observations, alone, is not particularly useful for making predictions, but that catalogue may be highly useful for testing hypotheses. One reason there are so many competing theories in the behavioral areas is that we don't have adequately measured and recorded data for testing them.

---

[16]Carl G. Hempel and Paul Oppenheim: The logic of explanation, in Herbert Feigl and May Brodbeck, eds.: *Readings in the Philosophy of Science*, New York, Appleton-Century-Crofts, 1953, p. 319.

[17]Brown: *op. cit.*, especially Ch. II.

Further, it may be doubted that any descriptions are as "mere" as they are sometimes taken to be. A description may involve not only a high degree of socialized experience, but perhaps fairly general theories. Dewey and Bentley emphasize what frequently is ignored:

> "Take two yellow cats and one black cat. Some little while afterwards, culturally speaking (a few tens of thousands of years, perhaps) primitive man will mark the color distinction, not as color for itself, but as color in contrast with other color. Put his color-naming in system with cat-naming, and you have the beginning of description."[18]

If descriptions are viewed in their cultural setting, then, and if the transactional nature of the process by which man differentiates various parts of nature is kept in mind, mere descriptions turn out to be rather complicated, and may indeed require explanation themselves as much as they help supply data for other explanations.

Transactionally viewed, then, an adequate description involves what many call explanation. Consider what Hempel and Oppenheim say about explanation:

> "It is this potential predictive force which gives scientific explanation its importance: only to the extent that we are able to explain empirical facts can we attain the major objective of scientific research, namely not merely to record the phenomena of our experience, but to learn from them, by basing upon them theoretical generalizations which enable us to anticipate new occurrences and to control, at least to some extent, the changes in our environment."[19]

Suppose we take a favorite example, a stick partially submerged in water that appears to be bent. Some, I imagine, would refer to this appearance as a "mere" description. But if what is here called an adequate description is given, in terms of light refraction, human perception, human language habits, etc., then such a description merges with explanation. Ideally, such an inquiry would result in warranted "if—then" assertions about those circumstances under which "normal" observers perceive certain types of phenomena.

---

[18]John Dewey and Arthur F. Bentley: *Knowing and the Known*, Boston, Beacon Press, 1949, p. 161.

[19]Hempel and Oppenheim: *op. cit.*, p. 323.

Frequently, then, it may be misleading to distinguish "description" sharply from "explanation." The reports given of what supposedly are sheer descriptions may involve a great amount of interpretation, and those interpretations may result partially from what is already accepted as proper explanation. On the other hand, a fully adequate description of the circumstances under which B follows A may itself be taken as an explanation of the occurrence of B.

Some people, however, seem to have a low opinion of any scientific explanation whatever. MacIver, in criticizing Gibson, says Gibson "really believes that we have satisfactorily explained why anything happens whenever we have said that such things always (or even only usually) happen."[20] Perhaps others will share MacIver's point of view, but I find it strange. What better explanation could we possibly have than that B always follows A under specified circumstances? To continue to ask "why?" after it is known that A is always followed by B can become pathological.

MacIver's comments raise some interesting points. It may be difficult to know that we actually have found regularities in behavior. We can also speculate as to how long the regularities will persist, or over what range they apply. Very often we may want a more detailed and precise analysis of observed regularities. To illustrate, a standard automobile will not run without a source of electric current. Although for some purposes a sufficient explanation of a given car's failure to operate will consist in pointing out that the battery is dead, we may also want a more detailed explanation in terms of the structure of an internal combustion engine. And that more detailed explanation can be supplemented by an even finer-meshed account, etc. The level of detail required of an explanation depends on the context. All that is here affirmed is that if we do have assurance that a certain regularity does hold, we have at least the beginning of a suitable explanation.

Suppose, to take a false example, a specified kind of aggression always follows a certain kind of frustration. Suppose further that Mr. James exhibits the relevant kind of aggression after being frustrated. If we know that such aggression always follows such frustration, don't we have a perfectly good explanation? Have we said anything

---

[20]MacIver: *op. cit.*, p. 272.

more useful if instead we give an "inner" account of what James feels like, and say what his intentions, motives, purposes, etc., were? If we put ourselves imaginatively in his position, and then see that we too would feel aggressive, have we answered the "why?" question any better than if we subsumed James' behavior under appropriate warranted generalizations? Since MacIver has said the aim of the kind of process he supports is not prediction, but understanding, we cannot invoke the superiority of scientific explanation for predictive purposes against him. But we may wonder why anyone would be so enamored of empathetic understanding that he would elevate its significance over that of reliable prediction.

Peter Winch, in his criticism of "hard science" approaches, emphasizes the importance of a philosophic analysis that reveals "what it makes sense to say."[21] Such understanding could be construed in the narrow sense of being in conformity with the rules of some language. It is frequently assumed these days by philosophers that ordinary language in some significant sense is "correct." But surely it is relevant and important to ask some questions about the rules of the language, such as whether they lead us to postulate dubious entities.

What it makes sense to say, moreover, can be viewed in other contexts. I would be inclined, for example, to say that what it makes sense to utter often depends on the regularities found in nature. Thus it no longer makes sense, in one way, to talk about the "ether" as classically construed, although it is obviously possible to discuss that term intelligibly. Language developed in prescientific times may lead one to accept entities that cannot be found, and because a term "properly" occurs in an utterance is hardly a sufficient warrant that anything corresponding to it occurs in the world. We can discourse perfectly well about dragons, but I think we would turn to zoology rather than our sensitivity to language to find out if any dragons inhabit our world.

Here again, then, the issue comes back to a question of verification. What distinguishes scientific description-explanation is that it has been empirically confirmed. Nonscientific explanations may be plausible and subjectively pleasing, but still may be only charm-

---

[21]Peter Winch: *The Idea of a Social Science and its Relation to Philosophy*, London, Routledge & Kegan Paul, 1958, p. 72.

ing "if-so" stories. As the psychologists George Mandler and William Kessen say, in their discussion of prominent literary figures:

> ". . . they may even provide a prodigality of plausible initial statements in their building of convincing portraits, but they and the nonempirical psychologists in general, apparently never feel the sharpest goad of the research psychologist—to find out by looking whether or not he is right."[22]

b) **Explanation and Prediction.** Considerable literature exists as to whether there is a logical symmetry or strong similarity between explanation and prediction. Much of it was generated by Hempel and Oppenheim's argument that "an explanation is not fully adequate unless its explanans, if taken account of in time, could have served as a basis for predicting the phenomenon."[23] The purpose here is not to review that literature in detail, nor even technical modifications of the thesis. Rather, it is to discuss views that explanation and prediction differ in behavioral inquiry and physical inquiry. However, the variety of ways in which "explanation" is used again needs emphasis. Disregarding technical disputes about the logical structure of prediction, it seems clear that often what people call an explanation does indeed have the same structure as prediction. But other uses of "explanation" may involve a different logical structure. A basic question, then, is what is to be counted as an explanation.

Olaf Helmer and Nicholas Rescher see a difference in the type of reasoning used in the *exact* and the *inexact* sciences. The difference between the two types of sciences is one of degree, not principle, and inexactness is not restricted to the behavioral fields. They characterize an inquiry as scientific if its purpose is the explanation and prediction of phenomena "in a reasoned, and therefore intersubjective, fashion." In an exact science the reasoning is formalized in that the terms used are "exactly defined" and the hypothesis is

---

[22]George Mandler and William Kessen: *The Language of Psychology*, New York, Wiley, 1959, p. 250.

[23]Hempel and Oppenheim: *op. cit.*, p. 323. A later paper of Hempel's, in Robert G. Colodny, ed.: *Frontiers of Science and Philosophy*, Pittsburgh, University of Pittsburgh Press, 1962, is also of interest. He argues against those who see an opposition between historical and scientific explanations.

derived in a logico-mathematical way from the evidence. In contrast, the corresponding reasoning in the inexact fields is informal. They say "in particular, some of the terminology may, without actually impeding communication, exhibit some inherent vagueness, and reasoning may at least in part rely on reference to intuitively perceived facts or implications."[24]

Although their warning about turning a difference of degree into a difference of kind is well taken, one may have reservations about the vagueness and the intuitiveness they mention. There is no doubt that such attributes characterize much work done under behavioral labels. But perhaps that should be deplored, not legitimatized; as Helmer and Rescher point out, some work done in the behavioral fields does not rely on what they call informal reasoning. What does seem central is the objective testing of hypotheses. Whether or not fully formalized derivations are used seems of considerably less importance. Surely there is a middle ground between fully formalized procedures and reliance on intuitions.

Some have argued that we can give good explanations of human behavior without using generalizations, laws, or theories. Theodore Mischel, for example, argues that successful literary works often produce such explanations. In discussing why Iago plotted against Othello, Mischel says:

> "Shakespeare is explaining why Iago acted in this way, but he is not saying anything about how all men, or all men of a certain kind, act under specified circumstances. To think that Shakespeare must have assumed that all men, or all vain, envious men, will act as Iago did under the circumstances would be silly—for such assumption is patently false."[25]

He goes on to argue that human actions puzzle us when we do not understand the person's intentions. An explanation often consists in our discovering something either about the person or the situation that discloses the reason involved. Since goal seeking behavior often follows rules, the reason for the action in question

---

[24]Olaf Helmer and Nicholas Rescher: *On the Epistemology of the Inexact Sciences*, Santa Monica, Calif., The RAND Corporation, P—1513, 1958. The quotations are from pp. 1-2.

[25]Theodore Mischel: Psychology and explanations of human behavior, *Philosophy and Phenomenological Research*, *XXIII*:579-80, 1963.

may become clear if we understand the rules, which can be legal or social norms, strategies in playing games, etc. He also says:

> "When we explain human behavior in terms of laws or disposi-
> tions we explain from 'outside,' in terms of regularity rather than
> rationale, in a way similar to that in which we explain the behavior
> of animals and things. But when we explain in terms of reasons we
> take the agent's point of view and look for the considerations which
> lead him to choose this deed as the right thing to do under these
> circumstances—in this sense we explain his behavior from 'in-
> side.' "[26]

Readers may use very different criteria when judging that an author has successfully shown his characters acting in certain circumstances. But would not many people regard an explanation as successful only if it conforms to the relevant generalizations they accept about human behavior? If a specified type of human in a specified context did not act in the way we think would be typical of all (or nearly all) such people under those circumstances, an explanation of that deviation would be required. We may not, of course, formally invoke generalizations from a sociology text, or cite something from the *Nebraska Symposium on Motivation*, but how can we know what a "rationale" might be, unless we relied on some generalizations about certain types of human behavior? In harmony with much of what Mischel says, if we knew nothing about Indian culture, we might be greatly surprised about the way a Hindu reacts to the sight of a large juicy piece of beef being roasted.

Interestingly enough, some of the examples given by Mischel also might be used by his opponents to illustrate their thesis. This can happen because Mischel insists on a basic distinction between reasons, on the one hand, and causes or dispositions, on the other. This has become a rather popular topic of discussion for phil-osophers recently, and it may be fair to summarize the situation as simply one in which many people see no radical distinction where others do. So again, we need to ask "What is it all for?" If we emphasize prediction, then perhaps we can compare, at least roughly, the success of scientific predictions with that of some other kind. If we reject predictions as the test, then we get involved in other matters on which humans hold widely varying opinions.

[26]*Ibid.:* p. 582.

5. INVESTIGATIVE PROCEDURES AFFECT WHAT IS BEING INVESTIGATED

Sometimes it is argued that the investigative techniques used in studying human behavior, the ideas held by the inquirer, the publication of the results, etc., affect what is being studied in a way that does not occur in the physical sciences. Peter Winch, for example, says that the conceptions used in social science "enter into social life itself and not merely into the observer's description of it," and that this constitutes a basic difference between the concepts of the two types of science.[27] In recent years perhaps most attention in this area has been devoted to "self-fulfilling" and "self-defeating" predictions. Even in the exact areas of physical science, it is said, predictions do not influence the behavior of what is forecast—presumably weather predictions do not influence the weather. But in human affairs predictions sometimes may either reinforce or tend to negate what is forecast. The rumor that there will be a sugar shortage may lead to sugar hoarding and thus help to produce what was predicted; dissemination of predictions that a given candidate will be elected may spur his opposition on to the point that the predicted winner will be defeated.[28]

It is doubtful whether any significant difference in scientific method flows from such considerations. As mentioned earlier, any prediction failing to take the relevant factors into account is likely to be unsuccessful. If the electorate has a tendency either to side with the underdog or to jump on the bandwagon, those tendencies need to be considered in making the prediction of the results of the election. As Gibson says:

> "In general it may be said that anyone who tries to make a prediction has to take account of any possible effects which the making of the prediction, or its publication, will have either on himself or on other people. Predictions which defeat themselves . . . are in no

---

[27]Winch: *op. cit.*, p. 95.

[28]For discussion of self-defeating and self-fulfilling predictions see Karl R. Popper: *The Poverty of Historicism*, London, Routledge & Kegan Paul, 1957, pp. 13-14; and Robert K. Merton: *Social Theory and Social Structure*, rev. ed., Glencoe, Ill., Free Press, 1957, Ch. XI. Two recent articles by philosophers may also be mentioned: Roger C. Buck: Reflexive predictions, and Adolf Grünbaum: Comments on Professor Roger Buck's paper: 'Reflexive predictions'. *Philosophy of Science*, *30*, 1963.

sense logically absurd, they are merely inadequate. . . . The case of self-fulfilling beliefs may be accounted for in the same say. In this case a prediction, made on the basis of *some* evidence . . . could have been supported by much better evidence if the predictor had realized that others (or he himself) on believing it would be stimulated to act in ways favourable to it."[29]

It is also well to recall that in the physical sciences the techniques or instruments used may influence the result. For example, as Scriven notes, Galileo was fortunate in the instruments available to him when he discovered the "law" of falling bodies:

> ". . . he had measuring instruments which were sufficiently sensitive to variations in the most recalcitrant variable (a waterclock reading to 1/10 of a 'pulse-beat') to reveal the law, while not so sensitive that they would yield the progressively greater inaccuracy as the absolute size of any variable increased (due to the mounting energy losses)."[30]

In short, a general problem in scientific methodology is the influence on the results of whatever is used in the inquiry, including the semantic system of the inquirer. Peculiarities in the behavioral area, although they do occur, are not such as to necessitate any modification in basic scientific method. Indeed, the most effective known way to allow for those peculiarities is to inquire scientifically into their role.

6. BEHAVIORAL SCIENCE QUESTIONS ARE A PRIORI CONCEPTUAL QUESTIONS

According to Winch, a mistake often made in contemporary social science is to take as empirical questions what actually are *a priori* conceptual questions. For him, philosophy consists in "the study of the nature of man's understanding of reality." He argues that sociology's central problem, to supply "an account of the nature of social phenomena in general," is philosophical.[31]

One can, of course, so define "sociology" that it is largely nonempirical. But certainly a vast number of the problems that be-

---

[29]Gibson: *op. cit.*, p. 204.

[30]Scriven: A possible distinction between traditional scientific disciplines and the study of human behavior, p. 335.

[31]Winch: *op. cit.*, pp. 40-43.

havioral scientists work on do not seem resolvable on the basis of the elucidation of "concepts." The correlation between slum housing and other behavior patterns is not likely to be found merely by an analysis of what is commonly meant by "slum," nor are the attitudes and actions of differing social strata likely to be uncovered by considering how we talk about such phenomena.

This is not to deny that some of the work of behavioral scientists may be generated much more by the terminology and intellectual framework used than by anything discoverable empirically. If someone postulates a system for exploring human behavior in which "minds" are taken as nonnatural entities, an elaborate framework of hypotheses could be developed, and much attention could be given to the relation of minds to brains, bodies, and other parts of the organism. But whether or not the system would be useful in predicting human thinking behavior is another question.

For illustrative purposes, let us consider the account of "rationality" by Helmer and Rescher. They set up four conditions for calling a person "rational." 1) Especially in betting, such a person has mutually consistent preferences, or is at least willing to correct those inconsistencies brought to his attention. 2) If no new relevant evidence is made available, he maintains reasonably stable personal probabilities. 3) New relevant evidence changes his personal probabilities in the "right" direction. 4) In those simple cases in which the evidence at his disposal is known, and the degree of confirmation of the hypothesis on the basis of the evidence is defined, his personal probability concerning the hypothesis conforms reasonably to the degree of confirmation. Particularly, they say, "he is indifferent as to which side to take in a bet which to his knowledge is a 'fair' bet."[32]

Probably no one would regard the foregoing account as an adequate elucidation of what "we" mean by "rational" in ordinary language, so no questions will be raised on that score. But the account may generate problems that would otherwise not arise. Are there any people who meet the criteria listed? Or do the criteria constitute an "ideal type" that observed behavior approximates? Can the results of theories based on the above notion of

[32]Helmer and Rescher: *op. cit.*, p. 26.

"rationality" be used to predict actual behavior? In short, some ways of specifying the use of terms may produce more problems than they solve.

The following seems typical of much that goes on in behavioral research: In the search for warranted assertions about behavior, the inquirers use and develop various notions. Those notions may facilitate research in the sense that they lead to the accurate measurement of change, an intersubjectively verifiable differentiation among aspects of the field of inquiry, reliable predictions, etc. They may at other times hinder research or prove useless, as in, for example, the reliance on a crude notion of "instinct" in earlier psychology. Many problems then, are both "empirical" and "conceptual." The ways in which we categorize, relate, and discuss the materials under study depend enormously on the semantic system used. A sharp distinction between the "empirical" and the "conceptual" does not seem useful. Rather we should realize their interrelation and be aware that our linguistic behavior itself (including our adjustive behavior through the use of language) can be scientifically studied.

7. SCIENTIFIC PREDICTION OF SOME SOCIAL EVENTS IS UNINTELLIGIBLE

Winch argues that human decisions cannot be *definitely* predicted, for "if they could be, we should not call them decisions."[33] He discusses several examples, and refers approvingly to an argument advanced by Maurice Cranston. Both Cranston and Winch argue that to predict the making of an invention or the composing of a poem would involve inventing the object or writing the poetry oneself, and hence that it is not possible to predict that someone else will do those things. Winch adds:

"It would be a mistake, though tempting, to regard this as a piece of trivial logic-chopping. One appears to be attempting an impossible task of *a priori* legislation against a purely empirical possibility. What in fact one is showing, however, is that the central concepts which belong to our understanding of social life are incompatible with concepts central to the activity of scientific prediction.

---

[33]Winch: *op. cit.*, p. 93.

> When we speak of the possibility of scientific prediction of social developments of this sort, we literally do not understand what we are saying. (We cannot understand it, because it has no sense.)"[34]

Issues relating to the correctness of ordinary language have already been discussed, so attention here will be restricted to the possibility of prediction. There may well be limits to certain kinds of predictions that can be made in the physical sciences, so even taking Winch's point at face value does not necessarily result in a sharp differentiation between the behavioral and physical sciences. The more important question is the extent to which the kind of "unintelligible" talk about prediction that Winch describes is characteristic of behavioral inquiry. And surely the attempt to predict the very first occurrence of something is a very minor part of the behavioral researcher's task. But something similar is done or might be done, such as attempting to describe the kind of circumstances under which it is likely a large number of inventions of a given type will be made. Even assuming Winch's conclusion is sound, then, the kind of activity shown to be unintelligible is not a major part of behavioral research.

Also, despite Winch's disclaimer that he is not attempting an *a priori* prohibition of an empirical possibility, behavioral predictions as here construed do not seem to be the kind of thing, in the main, that can be shown to be conceptually impossible. Whether we can arrive at warranted "if—then" assertions about particular types of behaviors is something that normally cannot be settled in advance.

8. CONCLUSION

Three rather elementary distinctions will help focus the present writer's point of view. First, we need to differentiate between scientific method in general (as discussed in the first three chapters) and the specific procedures, techniques, and methods used in various problem areas. Although the distinction is a commonplace one, it should not be forgotten. It is involved here because some who advocate natural science methods do not intend by that the *specific* methods used by, say, physicists, but rather their *general* methods.

---

[34]*Ibid.:* p. 94.

Many of the alleged differences between the physical and the behavioral fields discussed in this chapter have their merits, but they are here regarded as differences in specific techniques rather than differences in basic scientific methodology.

Secondly, we need to distinguish between the various and contrasting ways behavioral scientists now pursue their research, and alleged intrinsic impossibilities or limitations on scientific method as applied to behavioral inquiry. It is freely granted that much work actually done is not scientific, but it is also maintained that we do not have to accept this as a necessary fact for all time. Although debates as to what might or might not happen in the future are often inconclusive in the extreme, no arguments the present writer knows of that purport to show the impossibility or the gross limitation of scientific inquiry into human affairs, are to be taken very seriously.

Third, we should distinguish between those who maintain scientific method cannot be applied to human behavior and those who hold scientific accounts of human behavior are relatively trivial. Those who believe that explanations in terms of warranted generalizations about regular patterns of events are inferior to some other type of explanation can be found. Their preference may indicate a hostility to science in general, not just to behavioral science. Those, on the other hand, who think special circumstances preclude scientific research into many aspects of the affairs of men, although admitting that such research would be valuable if it were possible, can perhaps be more easily refuted.

In short, the position taken is that the relatively modest success to date of "hard science" techniques applied to the problems of men in society offers some ground for optimism about future success, and arguments directed against the possible use of such techniques seem implausible. One suspects that often the suspicion of science is not due to any intrinsic difficulty in exploring human behavior, but rather to the conviction that any such success would somehow lower the position of man, or make him a less exalted being than he is thought to be.[35]

---

[35]For an extreme attack on "scientism," see the essays in Helmut Schoeck and James W. Wiggins, eds.: *Scientism and Values*, Princeton, N. J., Van Nostrand, 1960.

7

THE "INFERIORITY" OF THE
BEHAVIORAL SCIENCES

1. WHAT IS INFERIORITY?

SOME critics maintain not only that behavioral inquiry is somehow basically different from physical inquiry, or that scientific
method has grave limitations when applied to human activity, but
also that the behavioral disciplines are inferior to the physical. Perhaps everyone can agree that a difference, although genuine, need
imply no superiority-inferiority relation. But even when people do
agree a superiority-inferiority relation is involved in a difference,
varying tastes and preferences may result in one person calling
"superior" what another regards as "inferior." On the whole, for
example, it has been a blessing for humanity that what one individual searches for in the way of a mate is not what everyone else
wants.

As Fritz Machlup, the economist, points out, often we are concerned about judgments of inferiority in cases where we can choose
among alternatives. For example, if we have a "free" choice and
find one textbook superior to another, that judgment has an important bearing on the choice we make. But presumably no one
would say we have that kind of choice between the physical and the
behavioral sciences. Even if it can be shown that the behavioral
fields are, in some specified sense, inferior to the physical fields,
that alone would constitute no reason for rejecting behavioral
science.[1]

---

[1]Fritz Machlup: Are the social sciences really inferior?, *The Southern Economic Journal*,
XXVII, 1961. (Presidential Address to the thirtieth annual conference of the Southern
Economic Association.) Many references are made to this essay in the present chapter,
and considerable use has been made of Machlup's summary of arguments alleging
the inferiority of behavioral research. Therefore, it may be well to emphasize that
many of the views expressed in this chapter are in disagreement with those of Machlup,
and it should not be assumed that the present chapter indicates either the tenor or
the substance of his thought.

Probably what is intended when the behavioral areas are said to be inferior is that, in terms of some particular notion of scientific inquiry, the behavioral sciences are considerably less developed than are the natural sciences. As is so frequently the case in controversies about the status of behavioral research, disagreements often are highly dependent on the question of what is taken as proper scientific method. We also find here shifts between discussions of what currently is being done in the name of behavioral research and what might be done in the future, or in principle.

Attention in the remainder of this chapter will be focused on views maintaining that there is a relatively clear, definite, and permanent difference in the kind of scientific precision possible, and in success in arriving at warranted assertions, between the two major categories. Our concern is methodological, then, and excludes other interesting questions about possible inferiorities in the caliber of practitioners and students in the various areas, the kind of social support and prestige given, etc.

2. MEASURABILITY OF PHENOMENA

Discussions sometimes center on questions in the theory of measurement, such as the adequacy of kinds of scales, or may concern the alleged recalcitrance of behavioral phenomena to numerical measurement. Our interest will be primarily with the former question. In relation to the latter, Machlup makes some important comments. As he points out, the sheer availability of massive amounts of data in numerical form may not be much of an advantage. Probably no empirical science has data "ready-made" in numerical form to a greater extent than economics, yet the raw data there must be adjusted and corrected, with many possibilities of error and a great expenditure of effort.[2]

In many behavioral areas, of course, the raw data are quantified only with great difficulty, and sometimes only crude quantification in terms such as "large," "small," "most," etc., typifies the work being done. But clearly similar problems occur in scientific areas other than the behavioral, and the latter fields often do have precisely quantified data at their disposal.

---

[2]*Ibid.*, p. 178.

The more serious allegation of inferiority revolves around the type of measurement possible, or at least presently available. It is frequently said that some of the physical sciences indulge in the luxury of "fundamental" measurement, but the behavioral sciences have achieved nothing comparable. Thus although an enormous number of scales for ordering and measuring behavioral phenomena have been developed, critics point out that these scales are seldom "additive." One unit of length added to another yields a length twice the magnitude of the original, but an I.Q. of 150 does not indicate twice the intelligence of an I.Q. of 75.

C. West Churchman has been extremely critical of the kind of criticism just mentioned. He maintains that additive scales are no more "fundamental" than other types of scale. What is important is that the experimenter "specify the formal properties of his scales."[3] To scale some property, he points out, is a way of giving information about the most efficient use of the property in a problem situation. "Control in measurement is for the sake of treating an object in the most effective manner relative to any problem." For example, in situations in which length is a critical factor, "the scaling of the length will provide us with all the information we have to know about the object with respect to its length in order to use it most effectively." Depending on the purpose then, nonfundamental or nonadditive scales may be perfectly satisfactory.

Churchman also challenges the view of Norman R. Campbell and others that there are "fundamental magnitudes," specified as those "the measurement of which does not depend on any other magnitude."[4] Very simple kinds of operation are involved in the determination of such magnitudes, and Campbell emphasizes the additive nature of the fundamental scales. Lengths, areas, weights, etc., are, according to him, all additive. As Churchman argues, it seems doubtful in the extreme to claim that the measurement of such magnitudes can be done independently of other magnitudes. In measurements of weight there are obvious questions about the

---

[3] C. West Churchman: A materialist theory of measurement, in Roy W. Sellars, V. J. McGill and Marvin Farber, eds.: *Philosophy for the Future*, New York, Macmillan, 1949, p. 488.

[4] Norman R. Campbell: *An Account of the Principles of Measurement and Calculation*, New York, Longmans, Green, 1928, p. 101.

accuracy of the balance and absence of convection currents. To investigate such questions, other measurements must be made.

Campbell further maintains that in the case of weighing, we "simply try out" various objects on the pans in order to check how well our operations conform to the formal conditions for additive magnitudes. In reply, Churchman says:

> "Well, how many objects must we try? Who shall try them? On what days? On the critical question of judging a result, Campbell asserts that the determination of lengths, for example, 'depends on judgments of the contiguity of parts of lines, which is a relation *instinctively perceived.*' Do all people instinctively perceive alike? Does one person instinctively perceive alike at different times?"[5]

Churchman emphasizes the problems that develop in laboratories in getting people to understand instructions in the same way, and insists on the grave difficulty of stating verbal instructions, no matter how simple they may seem, in a way that can be carried out in the same manner by even most workers.

Finally, Churchman stresses what here has been called the transactional approach. A precise measurement of the length of a line may presuppose ideal conditions. Thus we may be interested in knowing what the length of a line would be "ideally," if we could compare it to a standard meter rod, align the ends of the line exactly against marks on the meter rod, keep the temperature controlled, etc. We can only approximate such conditions, and hence we adjust the raw data to take account of well-established physical findings. There is then no reliance on what is "instinctively perceived" as basic, final, or fundamental. Rather both theory and practice are involved in the measurement even of alleged fundamentals. In Churchman's words:

> ". . . estimating what would happen in these idealized conditions requires all the science we have at our disposal; none of the so-called 'actual' operations we perform is basic, in the sense that we *infer* concerning the idealized environment from what is 'given.' The problem of what is actually given is itself only to be estimated; the pure given in experience is again an idealized experiment, just as the determination of a 'direct observation' requires setting up idealized conditions."[6]

---

[5]Churchman: *op. cit.*, p 484.

[6]*Ibid.*, p. 489.

The elevation of one kind of theory over practice occurs in a subtle form in many accounts of the logic of measurement. Discussion may be devoted almost exclusively to the question of the logical properties of certain kinds of scales, rather than to the adequacy of the scale in doing the job for which it was designed. It is often just assumed that a "neat and tidy" scale, in terms of its formal properties, will necessarily give equally "neat and tidy" results in the measuring process. In some cases, the very "perfection" of the scales may lead to a great many approximations having to be made during the process of measurement, and the errors resulting perhaps will be as troublesome, overall, as the problems associated with nonadditive scales.

To avoid misunderstanding, it may be well to emphasize here that no denigration of additive scales is intended. Their usefulness is obvious, and their introduction wherever possible is to be encouraged. What is objected to is the tendency to emphasize the formal properties of scales, and to rate various scientific inquiries on the basis of the kind of scale involved, rather than to stress the context in which the scales are used and their success or failure in doing their intended jobs. If, say, a certain I.Q. test can predict certain types of behavior with a high degree of reliability, we hardly need to lament that the difference between an I.Q. of 79 and one of 80 may be a different magnitude than that between scores of 109 and 110.

To summarize, perhaps both in terms of formal characteristics and successful use, the scales used in the physical sciences are usually superior to those in the behavioral sciences. But if one remembers the transactional nature of measurement in both areas of science and the concrete technological problems that arise, the differences, far from being fundamental, seem better viewed as instances in which physical scientists have handled their problems more adequately than behavioral scientists.

3. INVARIABILITY OF OBSERVATIONS

Two different types of "inferiority" have been discussed in this context. One is that chosen by Machlup, for example, in which the recurrence of repeatable regularities in nature is contrasted with the rapid change, the high degree of invariability, and the "unique" events of behavioral phenomena. Although Machlup thinks the difference is one of degree, he also maintains there is an important truth in that contrast, since only "a small number of reproducible facts will normally be involved in a physical explanation or prediction."[7] "Normally" here may prove to be troublesome; meteorology would seem to involve a great many factors, and we have very limited ability to reproduce them under controlled circumstances.

Perhaps more important is the question of the focus of analysis. An historian, for example, may be interested in the common features that can be abstracted from various revolutions that do differ from each other in important ways. Or a physical scientist may be concerned about the differences among processes that in general are highly similar. How we classify differences and similarities depends, of course, on the categories used. Quite often workers begin with the terminology of ordinary language. If an historian finds common features to what are often called revolutions, but finds these features missing in some processes also given that label, he may adopt a technical specification for the term so that it no longer conforms to ordinary language. If this process yields scientific success, it is to that extent justifiable. One suspects that more frequently in the behavioral areas than in other scientific areas, the layman demands or expects the scientist to "do justice" to all the uses of folk-language terminology. In short, what is taken as a regularity in the "external" world is highly dependent on the semantic system employed by the researcher. To assume that nature is, in some simple sense, divided into recurrent and unique events may be extremely naive.

The other type of inferiority discussed under the present topic deals with the allegedly great subjectivity and variation in observation characterizing studies of human behavior. Here the issues are closely related to those discussed in the previous section.

Churchman argues that great variations occur in supposedly simple observations in the so-called exact sciences. For example, when a variety of places make the same product, a great deal of energy may go into writing instructions for the measurement of the product's properties. Every so often different laboratories are asked

---

[7]Machlup: *op. cit.*, pp. 173-74.

to measure the same object, all of them supposedly following the same set of "precisely worded" instructions. According to Churchman the result "has almost always been that laboratories do *not* agree; sometimes they differ by amounts great enough to invalidate the whole process of inspection."[8] He mentions the "simple" operation of counting the number of grains in a well defined area of brass strip, and other similar instances, in which significant differences occurred in various laboratories.

What people take, then, as simple operations that are easily communicated and lead to a high degree of intersubjective agreement, may turn out less happily. Psychological work on perception shows how naive and inadequate many views on that topic are.[9] The danger, again, is to rely on some particular process, operation, or other form of human activity as something not subject to serious question, in the hope of constructing on that "firm" foundation other aspects of scientific inquiry. The temptation to say that something, at least, is beyond intelligent doubt, or the need for improvement, is a great one.

We also should not forget that many of the observations made in the behavioral sciences do lead to a high degree of intersubjective agreement, and replicable experiments are made. The enormous emphasis on standardizing tests and other tools of inquiry is worthy of mention. If we look at the agreement of observations as actually made, and not just at what follows from various notions about the contrast between observation in behavioral and other inquiries, we may not be so impressed by the differences in the invariability of measurement.

Again, there is no intention here to deny the high degree of intersubjective agreement commonly reached in the physical sectors of scientific inquiry, nor the need for the behavioral sectors to make more progress in that direction. The view urged here is that: a) We should not overemphasize the intersubjective agreement reached in

---

[8]Churchman: *op. cit.*, p. 485.

[9]For example, see Franklin P. Kilpatrick, ed.: *Explorations in Transactional Psychology*, New York, New York University Press, 1961. Although in opposition to much that is said here, and written from a very different perspective than the present monograph, Ch. I ("Observation") of Norwood Russell Hanson's *Patterns of Discovery*, Cambridge, At the University Press, 1958, is an interesting account of how seeing is often a "theory-laden" undertaking.

the physical sectors, or just assume that there are no problems; b) We should not underestimate the reliability of many procedures commonly used in the behavioral sectors; and c) We should not confuse paper simplicity, unambiguity, and absence of problems, with what goes on in the full process of scientific inquiry.

4. VERIFIABILITY OF HYPOTHESES

Some have urged that the kind of verification possible in the behavioral sciences is distinctly inferior to that achieved in the physical sciences. Behavioral scientists are plagued by a large number of conflicting hypotheses, it is said, and verification techniques are not available to resolve the issues, but in the physical sectors a constant winnowing out occurs, and the competition of theories is much less prominent. A major thesis of the present monograph is that something like this does happen; what we are interested in is the extent to which the situation can be remedied.

The simple distinction between *verifiability* and *verification* is relevant here. Some work done in studies of human behavior rests on hypotheses that either are, or come close to being, unverifiable in principle. But more important are hypotheses that, although veri*fiable*, have not been properly tested. The reasons for the lack of testing are various. Sometimes the difficulties of experimentation, human or technical, are involved. Sometimes the hypotheses developed are so far removed from any relevant data already collected or easily collectible that they remain untested. Available data frequently may be ignored. The academic barriers between disciplines may function so as to minimize communication of relevant results from one discipline to another. Or some basic assumption may be held so tenaciously that it forms an impenetrable seal against the findings of other disciplines.

Yet we need to remember that in the physical sciences, at any given time, there are likely to be many relatively untested hypotheses, and sometimes considerable passion goes into controversies about them. Especially in areas such as meteorology, where there is a very imperfect control over the variables, the same general kind of situation develops that characterizes much behavioral research. We also should recall that many hypotheses in behavioral work have been disconfirmed, and this is at least some progress.

In some cases, the critics may be chiefly interested in the range of the warranted assertions that are found in the behavioral fields. It has been argued that in the physical sciences "laws" are found applying to, for example, all electrons or all forces, but in the behavioral fields the generalizations apply only to relatively restricted groups. Warranted assertions about members of one socioeconomic or cultural group may not apply at all to members of a different group.

There is no doubt that people sometimes have far too much confidence in the universality of certain relations found to hold among various phases of the phenomena being investigated. We are tempted to project what is characteristic of the behavior of some people to all people. The tendency to overgeneralize about sign-behavior, which is not only complex, but affected by the sign-behavior of others, may be especially great. Yet the alleged inferiority of the behavioral fields in respect to range of hypotheses and generalizations is easily exaggerated, in terms both of its methodological and human significance.

Physical science "laws" also hold only within certain ranges. In many cases we need not worry about whether the proper conditions are met or not; normally, for example, we can assume no important change in the earth's gravitational field will occur while we are experimenting on falling bodies. But the findings, of course, would not hold if a significantly different gravitational field were involved. The "if" of the "if—then" form of warranted assertions is as important in the physical sector of science as in any other sector, in the sense that the consequent is predicted on the assumption that the antecedent occurs. Behavioral scientists, however, on many occasions have extreme difficulties in ascertaining whether or not their subjects are such as to conform to the required antecedent conditions.

Again attention should be called to the importance of the purpose of analysis. For a great many human purposes electrons can be considered as identical in all significant respects, and we seldom have reason to worry about those electrons "located" in Montana as compared to those in New York. Very often in studying humans we do need to take geographic differences into account, but sometimes we don't. What similarities and differences are relevant depends on the context of specific inquiries.

But even if we say the range of generalizations possible in the behavioral fields is very restricted compared to that in the physical fields, we cannot conclude that inquiries are bound to be more successful in the latter. For if we want to predict a given behavior pattern, what is important is that we have the requisite warranted assertions, not that the assertions used have a broad range. If we want to predict public opinion about the cessation of nuclear bomb testing, we need not worry about all humans or all cultures, but only about those whose opinion we want to predict. If we want to predict the results of an election, we need not be concerned about whether our generalizations apply to members of cultures other than the one involved. In short, what we want are generalizations that apply to what we are attempting to predict. If we can achieve that, the "breadth" of the range compared to that of some other generalization hardly seems a vital matter.

The general pattern of activity then, seems the same in all types of scientific inquiry. Hypotheses must be formulated in a way open to empirical testing. In all fields the reliable ascertainment of the data relevant to that testing may be a problem. As better instrumentation and ways of analyzing and collecting data are developed, what seemed to be a confirmation (or disconfirmation) of some hypothesis may turn out otherwise. The warranted assertions developed apply to specified circumstances. If we can predict what we are trying to predict with their aid, we have the "breadth" we need.

5. EXACTNESS OF FINDINGS

Discussions of "exactness" may concern several different things. The exactness of measurement may be what is referred to, and that has already been discussed. Or precision of prediction may be involved, and that will be discussed in the next section. Or the extent to which mathematical treatment is used may be of major concern. In addition to the senses just mentioned, Machlup also discusses another:

"The meaning of exactness best founded in intellectual history is the possibility of constructing a theoretical system of idealized models containing abstract constructs of variables and of relations between variables, from which most or all propositions concerning particular connections can be deduced."[10]

This type of exactness is lacking in some of the natural sciences, but is often found in economics and some parts of psychology, for example; and is dominant in many efforts in game theory, decision theory, cybernetics, general systems theory, and other recent developments.

Often there seems to be a strange confusion between the exactness of the derivations in such procedures, and the exactness of findings *relevant to human behavior*. Many of the alleged "breakthroughs" in behavioral science are praised for the exactness with which consequences can be drawn from the model. If it is objected that the results either are not useful predictions of human behavior, or that the assumptions made seem to conflict with well-established generalizations about that behavior, the defenders of the approach often show great impatience. In order to avoid distortion here, use will be made of extensive quotations from Anatol Rapoport.

He says, in referring to the mathematician who constructs "sociotheoretical mathematical models":

"He frequently cares little about the 'reality' of the underlying assumptions, not even about the referents of his terms. They are all 'as-if' terms and 'as-if' assumptions. His object is to deduce from these postulates relations among quantities which can be in principle verified. If he discovers relations which seem surprising in the sense that they would not have been ordinarily suspected but are nevertheless verified, he feels doubly rewarded. Often, not even the predictive power of the model is important. The model can have 'heuristic' value only."[11]

Later on, Rapoport says the mathematical worker often simplifies "situations beyond recognition," but this is necessary to begin the work. He continues:

"The social scientist should not demand realism from the mathematician's models but only pertinence. It is sufficient if the model contains the essentials, no matter how crudely simplified, of some

[10]Machlup: *op. cit.*, pp. 177-78.

[11]Anatol Rapoport: Uses and limitations of mathematical models in social sciences, in Llewellyn Gross, ed: *Symposium on Sociological Theory*, Evanston, Row, Peterson, 1959, pp. 354-55.

social process. The social scientist must therefore muster his intuitive powers to distinguish the salient features of the social process from the trivial."

He concludes that it "does not matter if the few salient features alone do not constitute a model which accurately describes or predicts. If the fundamentals have been captured, the work has started and can go on."[12]

Here we have an interesting example in which a rather cavalier attitude is tolerated toward the "intuitive powers" of the scientists to differentiate the important from the trivial, and a conviction that if the "fundamentals" have been grasped, the models, even when badly deficient initially, can be rectified.

But critics object that it is just the likelihood that our "intuitions" are wrong that demands our attention, and that to concentrate on the internal excellence of the model rather than its predictive ability may lead to a multitude of elegant but nonrelevant models. Frequently "ideal" but factually false laws from the physical sciences are cited in this context, as a kind of defense for behavioral models not conforming to observed behavior. But the merit of such "ideal" laws in an empirical science is that observed behavior at least approximates them. If those laws could not be used for prediction, after making suitable corrections, they presumably would not be retained. And for all we know, other ways of inquiring, not relying on ideal laws, might be developed that would give even better predictions.

The inability to control variables satisfactorily in many behavioral processes, then, may lead some to move to an area in which tight control can be maintained; that is, the making and developing of models. There is no necessary harm in this, and there may be considerable gain. But if the models do not help in the empirical business of science, the fixating on them just because their internal structure is attractive can impede scientific progress. In other words, in situations where we have no adequate way of predicting behavior, it can be tempting to construct elaborate and ingenious models; for example, game theory or cybernetic ones. If those models do not aid prediction, they still may be highly regarded for their charm. Some consolation is gained from the thought that if

---

[12]*Ibid.:* pp. 370-71.

any humans ever were found who act in a way corresponding to the models, we then would have a fine theoretical basis for studying their behavior.

In terms of logical coherence and similar criteria, I think there can be no doubt that behavioral workers have constructed models that are the equal of those found in the natural sciences. The behavioral areas are inferior in the sense that models there are usually less helpful in the accurate prediction of relevant behavior than their counterparts in physical science. But the main point is that in many areas it seems tempting to substitute control and prediction of the behavior of a model for control and prediction of the behavior supposedly under investigation.

6. PREDICTABILITY

Frequently it is said that physical scientists not only make far more successful predictions than do behavioral scientists, but also that the former's predictions tend to be much more accurate. Once again we find considerable looseness of expression. How should we measure the total number of successful predictions, what counts as a prediction, how accurate must it be to count as successful, how do we distinguish between trivial and important predictions, etc.?

As Machlup notes, the great success of the physical scientists has occurred in strictly controlled laboratory situations. The engineering applications, however, often meet many unexpected difficulties, and predictions about phenomena outside the laboratory context can be very inaccurate. Sometimes, he goes on, behavioral scientists are expected to foretell what will happen in situations comparable to ones in which not much is expected from physical scientists:

> "[Physical scientists] would never undertake to predict the number of fatalities in a train wreck that might happen under certain conditions during the next year. They do not even predict next year's explosions and epidemics, floods and mountain slides, earthquakes and water pollution. Social scientists, for some strange reason, are expected to foretell the future and they feel badly if they fail."[13]

Of course behavioral workers do make many predictions that are borne out with a high degree of accuracy. Many events that

---

[13]Machlup: *op. cit.*, p. 180.

we wish could be predicted cannot be, but that also characterizes other scientific areas. Perhaps it would not be too inaccurate to say that in situations allowing strict control, the kinds and accuracy of prediction in behavioral fields will stand comparison with that of other scientific fields. In all areas prediction tends to falter when one cannot be certain of either the occurrence, or the magnitude, of variables that influence the results. The measurement and the prediction of a falling body under laboratory conditions is quite another matter than the measurement and prediction of a falling leaf on a gusty day.

Sometimes a distinction is made between conditional and unconditional predictions, and it is thought that the physical sciences make at least some unconditional predictions, while the number of variables that must be taken into account in the behavioral sciences make even conditional prediction hazardous there. Machlup, for example, seems to think that physical scientists make some such unconditional predictions. In contrast, he argues, it is extremely difficult in economics, for example, to take account of the effects predictions may have on the behavior being predicted, as in self-defeating and self-fulfilling predictions.[14]

Perhaps "unconditional" is not being used here in as strong a sense we might assume. But if it is maintained that "unconditional" refers to predictions that something will happen at a given time, no matter what else happens, surely none of the scientific disciplines display such achievements. As mentioned earlier, physicists sometimes are able to predict without putting emphasis on the variability of antecedent conditions. In the case of eclipses, for example, we seldom fret about the possibility of a solar body being destroyed before the eclipse, nor do we normally worry about past regularities suddenly not holding. But this is far from "unconditional" in the sense of "no matter what else happens." To put the matter loosely, it seems clear that frequently in the physical sciences the number of variables in the "if" part of an "if—then" statement is smaller and less likely to escape effective control than in the behavioral sciences. Yet this is not always so; the prediction of the weather may be as difficult and as unsatisfactory as the prediction of many human actions. And as the behavioral sciences develop, they may yield more and more precise predictions.

---
[14]*Ibid.*

7. CONCLUSION

By now it must be rather dreary to read continually that existing differences are only of degree, not kind, or that genuine inferiorities are likely to be only temporary. The recurrence of that theme in the preceding sections, however, is deliberate, since so often it seems assumed by critics of the behavioral fields that present deficiencies are necessarily permanent. For all we know, of course, the future may show that even worse limitations than now imagined are in store for the behavioral sciences. Yet over and over statements of alleged inferiorities are coupled with the qualification that the same deficiency can be found in the physical sciences, but to a lesser extent. It is not some *a priori* conviction, then, but the parallels found, that results in the view that the same general methodological problems occur in all the sectors of scientific inquiry.

Of course, converging differences of degree can amount to a very genuine inferiority, and it is not denied here that in many relevant senses the behavioral fields are sadly inferior to the physical fields. The interesting and important questions, however, concern the relative fixity of those inferiorities; they are problems to be solved rather than intrinsic methodological differences. The present author, for example, finds it difficult to understand why some put so much methodological emphasis on self-defeating and self-fulfilling predictions. Empirically those processes are fascinating, but their elevation to profound methodological distinctions seems pointless. Can it be any more difficult to take account of the consequences a published prediction may have on those whose behavior is being predicted than it is to take account of the relevant variables in many of the difficult parts of physics and biology? And may not prediction of other aspects of human behavior be more difficult than allowing for the possible effects of the publication of predictions?

In many respects, then, achievements to date in the behavioral fields are inferior to what has been done in other scientific fields. Perhaps instead of devoting great efforts to "proving" that the tasks of behavioral science are so difficult that little can be expected, we might profit by looking outside technical methodological issues a moment in order to account for those inferiorities. Leslie White, for example, argues with a considerable show of evidence that scientific progress comes first, and develops most quickly, in areas in which the determinants of human behavior are least significant.[15] The relatively full-scale projection of human traits on the "external" world, common in earlier times, resulted in science developing first where that projection was weakest, in astronomy. Eventually, as animistic tendencies weakened, various other areas became open to scientific inquiry, and finally even cultural and symbolic behavior was attacked in a scientific manner.

The fear that scientific inquiry somehow will turn man into a mere object, dethrone him from his proper place in the cosmos, or otherwise endanger his ego, appears in many forms. It may be boldly and unequivocally stated by overt enemies of science, or it may intrude in milder form in accounts that formally claim allegiance to science. For an example of the latter, we might again mention those who insist not only that we must explain much (or most, or the "interesting" parts of) human behavior by giving an account of the motives of the humans involved, but who also think this constitutes a satisfactory explanation rather than (often) a tautology or near vacuous explanation.

Arthur F. Bentley's analysis, made as far back as 1908, deserves attention. He insisted that interpretations in terms of "the feelings and ideas" of the people involved in social behavior often block "explanation as much as the animism of the forest would block the study of nature."[16] He discusses in detail an example of a person who, on seeing a man bullying a boy, stops and knocks the bully down. When Bentley asked why the hero acted as he did, he was told that sympathy for others explained the action. Bentley asks why the "sympathy" is expressed in some social contexts, but not in others:

> "The man who got the praise from the crowd is known to me. Half a mile from where he lives there are women and children working their lives out for less than a nourishing living. Nearby an old woman starved to death a few days ago. Child-labor under most evil conditions is common in the city. A friend of his is making his wife's life a burden by day and a horror by night. Yet he does not intervene to save the starving, or to alleviate the condition of the

---

[15]Leslie A. White: *The Science of Culture*, New York, Grove Press, 1949, pp. 111-12.
[16]Arthur F. Bentley, *The Process of Government*, Bloomington, Ind., Principia Press, 1935 edition, p. 3.

half-fed workers. He does not join the society for the prevention of child-labor. He does not use his influence with his friend to show him the brutality of his ways . . . . When my friend said that sympathy had moved the man to his act, he did, then, but restate in other words the very question I had asked."[17]

Of course what people want, prefer, think, and believe is important in describing their behavior. What is objected to is only the tendency to take such motivational accounts as methodologically privileged, and to regard those "inner" processes as phenomena that cannot in turn be investigated in a scientific manner.[18]

---

[17]*Ibid.*, p. 6.

[18]For some fairly typical philosophic discussions of this issue, see Donald Davidson, Actions, reasons, and causes; V. C. Chappell, Comments; and W. D. Falk, Action-guiding reasons, all in *Journal of Philosophy*, LX, 1963.

8

TERMINOLOGICAL PROBLEMS

1. THE GENERAL SETTING

THE present writer cannot recall even one commentator on behavioral science terminology who was satisfied with the situation in his discipline. Observers often hold that there are major difficulties, and sometimes view the situation as chaotic. From time to time relatively large scale attempts are made to clarify and standardize terminology.[1] On the other hand, workers in behavioral areas often think terminological confusion is not serious; semantic analysis strikes them as far less important than research into substantive problems. In many instances, however, semantic confusion seems inextricably bound to substantive problems.

On occasion jargon and needlessly technical terms are used so profusely that sheer unintelligibility results. Daniel Bell's spoof, "The Parameters of Social Movements: A Formal Paradigm," deserves mention in this connection. Its opening paragraph reads:

> "The purpose of this scheme is to present a taxonomic dichotomization which would allow for unilinear comparisons. In this fashion we could hope to distinguish the relevant variables which determine the functional specificities of social movements. Any classifica-

---

[1]A few samples may be mentioned. In psychology two recent attempts are of interest: William S. Verplanck's *A Glossary of Some Terms Used in the Objective Science of Behavior*, Washington, D. C., American Psychological Association, 1957, and George Mandler and William Kessen's *The Language of Psychology*, New York, Wiley, 1959. Verplanck's effort was strongly criticized by many psychologists concerned with social and clinical materials, and the Mandler-Kessen approach is heavily tied to logical positivism, a view challenged by many. In economics, L. M. Fraser's *Economic Thought and Language*, London, Adam and Charles Black, 1947, is highly critical of much of the language of economists, but it does not seem to have made a great impact. John Dewey and Arthur F. Bentley's *Knowing and the Known*, Boston, Beacon Press, 1949, proposes a group of trial names to be used in studying human sign-behavior, but very little attention has been given to it. In general, the sad situation is that very few attempted reforms have had much success.

tory scheme is, essentially, an answer to some implicit other scheme. In this instance, it is an attempt to answer the various hylozoic theories which deny that social categories can be separable."[2]

His parody is almost too good, and one suspects that many who have waded through vast realms of behavioral science material would not be put off in the slightest by the passage quoted. Bell says he sent his spoof to two sociologists he thought would appreciate it. One replied seriously about some of the categories, and the other, uncertain as to Bell's intentions, wrote: "You are too good a sociologist not to have created something which itself is quite useful."

Fairly common are writings that, although intelligible, bristle with special terminology used by only one author or by a small group. Sufficient attention to such terms may allow one to understand what is said, and the material communicated may be important. In a given discipline, varieties of competing nomenclature are typically found, and identical or very similar problems are discussed in different disciplines by means of widely varying terminology.

Perhaps most serious of all, as illustrated below, is the prominent use of nomenclature that impedes inquiry, suggests that the findings have a much wider relevance than they actually have, or misleads others as to possible applications.

2. SOME EXAMPLES OF TERMINOLOGICAL PROBLEMS

In this section only a few examples are discussed. The verbal snarls chosen are not alleged to be the most important, but were selected to illustrate certain types of problems commonly encountered in the behavioral sciences.

The terms "specify" and "specification" are used here where most literature would refer to "define" and "definition." The reasons for avoiding the use of "definition" are basically those given by John Dewey and A. F. Bentley.[3] "Specification" is used in this

---

[2]Daniel Bell: The parameters of social movement: a formal paradigm, anthologized in Dwight Macdonald, ed.: *Parodies: An Anthology from Chaucer to Beerbohm—and After*, New York, Random House, 1960, pp. 491-92.

[3]Dewey and Bentley: *op. cit.*, Ch. VII. Their account of some problems associated with "definition" has been much neglected.

monograph to refer to the efficient kind of designation found in scientific inquiry.

a) Information. Information theory was, and still sometimes is, heralded as a major "breakthrough" in behavioral science. Many attempts were made to apply the results of information theory to the older behavioral disciplines. Quite often it was assumed that a reliable way of measuring the content of information in a given message was now available, and that human communication at last could be described and measured scientifically.

As Yehoshua Bar-Hillel has shown, much foolishness stemmed from a relatively simple confusion between two senses of "information." In the development of the theory by communication engineers, "information" was given a restricted and technical specification. The communication engineers were interested in coding, transmitting, and receiving messages in relation to some specified speed of transmission, accuracy of transmission, and economic cost. For example, the frequency of the sequence t-h-e of all three-letter sequences in English was important for their concerns. Precise measures were developed in which "information" referred only to the *statistical rarity* of certain kinds of signal sequence transmissions. However, as Bar-Hillel points out, psychologically one is almost impelled to shift from this technical sense to the more usual sense; that is, "information" taken as what the signal sequence expresses. Thus we have estimates made of the "amount of information" in a Sunday copy of the *New York Times*, etc.[4]

The taking of "amount of information," in the technical sense, as synonymous with "amount of meaning" (ignoring, for the moment, all problems about the meaning of "meaning") has not only tempted the non-expert, but also those closely involved with the development of information theory.[5] The meritorious desire of information theorists to handle problems of communication and "meaning" in a scientific manner sometimes blinded them to the limitations of what had been achieved, or made them assume that

---

[4]Yehoshua Bar-Hillel: An examination of information theory, *Philosophy of Science*, 22:1955.

[5]Norbert Wiener, for example, takes "amount of information," as synonymous with "amount of meaning," in *The Human Use of Human Beings*, Boston, Houghton Mifflin, 1950, pp. 7-8.

their results were at least the beginnings of a scientific study of communication in the broad sense.[6]

As mentioned earlier, the availability of techniques sometimes results in their application to materials inappropriate, or only marginally appropriate, for investigation by those techniques. Disillusionment is likely to develop if that occurs, and genuine achievements may be underestimated. Much disillusionment with information theory is based on mistaken applications and exaggerated claims, not on defects within the theory.

b) Culture. The central place of "culture" in anthropological writings has resulted in many attempts to specify that term. Clyde Kluckhohn and A. L. Kroeber found some 164 definitions of "culture," all different and many contradictory.[7] Although many anthropologists do not seem disturbed by such disagreement, and although it may be easy to exaggerate its significance, the amount of disagreement suggests that some important issues are involved.

Perhaps the major issues concern the delimiting of anthropology from related disciplines, and the types of relation thought to obtain among those disciplines. A. R. Radcliffe-Brown and Leslie White represent two extreme views. Radcliffe-Brown holds that "a science of culture" is impossible, and that culture can be studied only "as a characteristic of a social system." The science, if there can be one, must be a science of social systems.[8] White, on the other hand, maintains that "culturology" is a separate field to be distinguished from other behavioral sciences. Culture traits exist before the individual is born, and act from outside the individual just as do meteorologic forces. Cultural phenomena cannot be "reduced" to anything else; culture *qua* culture can only be explained in cultural terms.[9]

---

[6]Thus Warren Weaver uses "communication" to refer to "all of the procedures by which one mind may affect another," which involves music, art, theatre, "and in fact all human behavior." He goes on to say that sometimes a still broader notion may be desirable. Claude Shannon and Warren Weaver: *The Mathematical Theory of Communication*, Urbana, University of Illinois, 1959, p. 95. See also pp. 114-17 for his optimistic view of what may develop from existing information theory.

[7]A. L. Kroeber and Clyde Kluckhohn: *Culture: A Critical Review of Concepts and Definitions*, Cambridge, Mass., Papers of Peabody Museum, 1952.

[8]A. R. Radcliffe-Brown: *A Natural Science of Society*, Glencoe, Ill., Free Press, 1957, p. 106.

[9]Leslie White: *The Science of Culture*, New York, Grove Press, 1949, pp. 78-79.

Although there may be considerable agreement in the way anthropologists actually use "culture" (for example, agreement in differentiating culture traits from other traits), the disagreements about the most adequate specification of that term reflect both methodological and empirical issues. Do cultural phenomena constitute a separate level of human behavior, and what is meant by "level?" Can all, or some, such phenomena be explained in social and/or psychological terms? How are cultures and societies related?

c) **Utility.** Some of the literature referred to here on "utility," as well as on "rationality" in d) below, was discussed earlier in another context (Chapter 2, Section 9, "Some Examples of the Failure to Unite Theory and Laboratory Work").

Traditional economists often relied heavily on the notion of utility, understood roughly as the ability to satisfy a want. Attempts to use that notion often generated more difficulties than they solved. In recent years a revised and supposedly improved notion of utility has had considerable currency in game theory. But some of the same old problems arise concerning both the identification and the measurement of utilities in observed human behavior. Often a utility approach is relied upon because it allows the development of an elegant mathematical framework. John von Neumann and Oskar Morgenstern, it will be recalled, assumed utilities were numerical, as well as substitutable and transferable without restriction among the players in the game, because "numerical utilities were needed for the theory of the zero-sum two-person game" and "substitutability and transferability were necessary for the theory of the zero-sum n-person game."[10]

Other writers have pointed out the dangers of identifying a player's utility with some numerical measure that occurs in the game. In gambling situations, perhaps some players want to maximize their expected money gain, and in such cases the identification of utility with expected gain would be proper. But if other players enjoy the thrill of bluffing, their utilities may not be at all in accord with expected money payments.[11]

---

[10]John von Neumann and Oskar Morgenstern: *Theory of Games and Economic Behavior*, 3rd ed., Princeton, Princeton University Press, 1953, p. 604.

[11]See, for example, R. Duncan Luce and Howard Raiffa: *Games and Decisions*, New York, Wiley, 1957, p. 5.

Other problems might be mentioned, but it seems evident that the desire to work out in considerable detail the solutions to various types of games has led to the introduction of utilities for which observable referents in human behavior may not be available, and that what people try to maximize may not be easily measurable. Putting the matter another way, if game theory is taken as an attempt to describe and predict human behavior, "utility" may be more a problem to be explained than an aid in explanation.

The present writer is well aware that the above problem can in a sense be disposed of, as are many similar problems, by saying that "utility" is a hypothetical construct. Without going into detail about controversies relating to such constructs, it may be observed that to handle problems by giving them an impressive label is a nice bit of word magic. If the use of utilities led to accurate predictions of human behavior, then the peculiar status of those utilities might be tolerated. But the failure of game theory to predict observed behavior perhaps rests partly on the use of "utility" and other notions, the primary function of which seems to be their service in the elaboration of nicely worked out theory. That some supporters have given up viewing game theory as descriptive, and now regard it as a normative or prescriptive account of how rational players should behave, is of interest in this context.[12]

d) **Rationality.** The use of this term in game and decision theories (as well as in economics and some other fields) results in problems similar to those concerning "utility." Kenneth J. Arrow, for example, mentions that "rational behavior" is often taken as referring to what the inquirer postulates as behavior describable in terms of an attempt to maximize some quantity.[13] R. Duncan Luce and Howard Raiffa, after commenting on ambiguities and imprecision in the use of "rational," say that loosely it includes assumptions made about players maximizing something, and "complete" knowledge of the players about the aspects of a complex situation.

---

[12]See, for example, Anatol Rapoport: *Fights, Games, and Debates*, Ann Arbor, University of Michigan Press, 1960, pp. 226-27; and Patrick Suppes and Richard C. Atkinson: *Markov Learning Models for Multiperson Interactions*, Stanford, Stanford University Press, 1960, p. 33.

[13]Kenneth J. Arrow: Mathematical models in the social sciences, *General Systems*, 1:33, 1956.

They go on to say that "experience" shows that actual humans would be far more restricted in what they know.[14] (For example, it may be assumed that all players are fully informed about the preference patterns of the other participants.)

Very often the use of "rational" is that demanded by some particular theoretical solution. Thus Anatol Rapoport says "we will use . . . a definition to suit a situation." For example, it is assumed that a rational man, faced with mutually exclusive alternatives, can arrange those alternatives in a preference order, perhaps allowing for indifference among alternatives.[15]

Sometimes, as noted earlier, a theory is taken not as a descriptive account of behavior, but as a normative account of what a rational man would do. Robert L. Davis regards both "normative" and "rational" unfortunate in such contexts. For the theories do not actually tell the alleged rational man what he *should* do, but rather specify *one* way in which the expected pay-off can be maximized. The maximum expected pay-off might be obtained more easily in other ways. Usually modern normative theory says in effect: "If a person's behavior is such that under the proper interpretation it can be said to satisfy the requirements of this system, then his behavior is what is called 'rational' in my theory."[16]

Some of the attraction decision theory has had stems from the belief that at last an objective and well-substantiated method is available either to describe or prescribe rational behavior. Since so many humans take pride in man's supposed rationality, see it as the *differentia* between man and other species, etc., they may become enamored of approaches promising, or seeming to promise, some leverage on rational behavior. But clearly, and independently of other difficulties with the notion, "rationality" as used in the contexts discussed above seems quite different from many of the uses of that term in ordinary discourse.[17] Far from adding insight into what

---

[14]Luce and Raiffa: *op. cit.*, p. 5.

[15]Anatol Rapoport: Introduction, in Dorothy Willner, ed.: *Decisions, Values and Groups*, New York, Pergamon Press, 1960, Vol. 1, p. xiv.

[16]Robert L. Davis: Introduction, in R. M. Thrall, C. H. Coombs, and R. L. Davis: *Decision Processes*, New York, Wiley, 1954, pp. 4-5.

[17]Paul Diesing, for example, argues against the extension without modification of certain technical notions and arguments to social, legal, and political problems. See especially the opening pages of his *Reason in Society: Five Types of Decisions and Their Social Conditions*, Urbana, University of Illinois Press, 1962.

is often called rational behavior, then, decision theorists may be adding a technical use of "rational" to those of common usage.

e) Morpheme. Some interesting points may be observed about the ways linguists attempt to specify "morpheme." As units of languages, morphemes are in a sense reminscent of words, but of course are not to be identified with them. (What a *word* is, in a language, can be specified in terms of phonemes and morphemes.) For example, in the following sentence, hyphens indicate the morpheme divisions: The-cat-s-are-purr-ing. Apparently there is excellent agreement among linguists as to what the morphemes of a given language are.

Quite often "morpheme" is discussed in relation to "meaning": morphemes are said to be "minimal semantic units" or the "smallest elements having meaning."[18] Questions of meaning are almost always vexing, and often the linguists who attempt to specify "morpheme" in terms of "meaning" rush on to other matters without saying much that is illuminating about their use of the latter term. Probably to avoid bogging down in discussion of the "meaning of meaning," some linguists specify "morpheme" in terms of a *class* of "related, recurring events."[19]

If, as mentioned, there is a high degree of agreement about identifying morphemes, it may seem pointless to worry very much about the formal characterizations offered for that term. But some frequently encountered "definitions" illustrate that terms having important scientific uses may be difficult to specify, and that further confusion may be produced by introducing highly troublesome terms in the supposed specification. Possibly, too, some of the difficulty relates to current debates within technical linguistics as to the extent linguists should try to deal with "meaning." Some advocate a purely formal approach independent of so-called semantic problems and the adjustive behavior of humans by means of

---

[18]See, for example, Roger Brown: *Words and Things*, Glencoe, Ill., Free Press, 1958, pp. 50-51; John Lotz: Linguistics: symbols make man, in Lynn White, Jr., ed.: *Frontiers of Knowledge in the Study of Man*, New York, Harper, 1956, p. 218; and John B. Carroll: *The Study of Language*, Cambridge, Harvard University Press, 1959, p. 24.

[19]As does Henry Lee Smith, Jr., for example, in his Linguistics: a modern view of language, in Lyman Bryson, ed.: *An Outline of Man's Knowledge of the Modern World*, New York, McGraw-Hill, 1960, p. 362.

language. Others think linguistics should be much concerned with those problems.[20]

f) Sovereignty. There is an extensive literature in political science on this term. It often has been used to refer to some kind of indivisible supreme will, or to the person or group of persons whose commands receive obedience. The notion of indivisibility was challenged by some critics. Debates as to whether sovereignty was conferred by consent or force occurred, and some commentators thought the question misleading. Legal and political sovereignty have been distinguished, although that distinction also has been alleged to make little sense. Sovereignty was said to have a kind of stability that government lacked; sovereign states continue although governments change.[21]

The notion of sovereignty has often struck critics as being a classic example of hypostatization. Governmental processes are fairly easy to identify, but when certain distinctions are made between "sovereign state" and "government," problems seem to multiply. Although it is helpful to have terms to refer to the difference, for example, between relatively durable institutions and the more rapid changes in party control, the critics maintain that the traditional notion of sovereignty unfortunately tended to direct attention toward some mythical entity. What was of merit in the notion is better discussed in terms of the actions of officials, institutional processes, etc. A. F. Bentley, for example, held that although the term may serve as a weapon in defense of existing governments or as a rationalization of policies and actions, "as soon as it gets out of the pages of the law-book or the political pamphlet, it is a piteous, threadbare joke."[22]

Clearly this is not the place to attempt a review of even the major competing notions of sovereignty, nor of the controversy surrounding the uses of that term. However, it may be cited as an example of

[20]A helpful, brief, and relatively nontechnical account of some of these controversies is given by Joseph H. Greenberg: Language and linguistics, in Bernard Berelson, ed.: *The Behavioral Sciences Today*, New York, Basic Books, 1963.

[21]A good brief account of many of these issues is given by G. C. Field: *Political Theory*, London, Methuen, 1956, Chs. IV, V.

[22]Arthur F. Bentley: *The Process of Government*, Bloomington, Ind., Principia Press, 1935 ed., p. 264.

a term loaded with various connotations stemming not only from traditional political philosophy, but from diverse ideological disputes. This is of course not to deny the obvious, that someone could so stipulate the term as to allow for its functioning in scientific discourse about human political behavior. Rather it is to point out that some terms are likely to produce many quarrels, misunderstandings, and unenlightening controversies, even if valiant efforts are made to rescue them for scientific use.

g) Control. Writers on cybernetics are fond of the term "control." Cybernetics is frequently said to be the science of control and communication, or the study of the control systems of all communication systems, human or otherwise. Rather rapid shifts from the sense of "control" in which a thermostat regulates room temperature, to the sense in which a dictator controls his populace, are sometimes made. Norbert Wiener, for example, is much concerned over humans becoming victimized by machines, especially since better machines are becoming available.[23] On the other hand, some writers have been concerned to avoid certain senses of "control." Stafford Beer, for example, says the term is not "used in the way in which either an office manager or a gambler might use it; it is used as a name for connectiveness."[24]

The type of control exercised by feedback mechanisms seems different in important respects from someone or something forcing humans to do what they don't want to do. Surely even the most generous estimate of the possibilities of cybernetics does not include a study of *all* the ways in which humans are "controlled." The describing of cybernetics as a science of control may be quite plausible in terms of certain types of what is commonly called control, but not for other types.

h) Values. In recent years scientists from many disciplines have turned their attention to a scientific attack on "values," in the hope of avoiding some of the problems associated with traditional inquiries. Vagueness and ambiguity abound in these scientific attempts. Studies into what people say they want or like, what goals

---

[23]Norbert Wiener: The brain and the machine (Summary), in Sidney Hook, ed.: *Dimensions of Mind*, New York, New York University Press, 1960, p. 114.

[24]Stafford Beer: *Cybernetics and Management*, New York, Wiley, 1959, p. 9.

they profess, their ideals, etc., are said to be investigations of "values." Experiments have been conducted to see what choices among alternatives are made in gambling and other situations. Attitude scales are constructed, content-analyses have been made of literature and other media, etc. Sometimes a distinction similar to Dewey's between the *desired* and the *desirable* is carefully adhered to, but at other times no such distinction is made. In some questionnaires there is almost no control over certain aspects of the inquiry. Whether people regard their responses to the questions as accurate indications of what they would choose, what they think they should choose, or what they think would be preferred by some social group, is uncertain.

The diversity of the ways in which "value" has been used in nonscientific contexts also complicates the matter. The many referents for value terminology in traditional approaches as well as in the newer empirical approaches make it practically impossible to say in what way a scientific conclusion might relate to the settling of traditional controversies. Hence to say that a given study has shown such and such relation between the subjects' values and other aspects of their behavior may not communicate very much. The expectations of the reader combined with unclarity as to what has been investigated may make it seem that far more has been achieved than actually was.

None of the foregoing should be understood as suggesting that a scientific investigation of human preferential behavior is either impossible, unfruitful, or inadvisable. But until such investigators say more clearly just what it is they have inquired into, their statements about their conclusions are almost certain to be misunderstood.

i) Intelligence. No attempt will be made here to review even the major disputes surrounding the most adequate specification of "intelligence." Charles C. Spiker and Boyd R. McCandless show rather convincingly that many of the disputes derive from terminological confusion; their analysis gives rise to some further problems that will be discussed here.[25]

---

[25]Charles C. Spiker and Boyd R. McCandless: The concept of intelligence and the philosophy of science, *Psychological Review*, *61*, 1954.

The authors were strongly influenced by logical positivism, and emphasize Gustav Bergmann's distinction between meaning I (formal, operational meaning) and meaning II (significance, usefulness, fruitfulness).[26] Spiker and McCandless maintain that useful scientific terms have both types of meaning. They argue that scientists who make use of common sense terms need not try to include all the ordinary language connotations. They suggest that much of the hue and cry about I.Q. stems from different inquirers focusing on different ordinary language connotations of "intelligence." Spiker and McCandless believe that common sense uses of the term lead to logical contradiction, and for this reason (among others) the psychologist is not obliged to try to measure all the things to which "intelligence" commonly refers.

They also are highly critical of the literature on "culture-free" intelligence tests, which they believe confuses value and factual matters. Specifically, they mention the approach of Kenneth W. Eells and his co-workers.[27] The Eells' group maintains that middle-class notions of what is best and true are incorporated into many intelligence tests, and lower-class children are penalized when they take such tests. Items to be recognized on the tests may be much more frequent in middle-class surroundings than in lower-class surroundings; for example, certain musical instruments. Although intelligence tests often predict school success very well, they do not measure the general problem solving abilities of people. The development of a test to measure the latter would help to prevent social class prejudice, discrimination, etc., and show that there are no class differences in genetic intellectual equipment. Eells' is critical not only of intelligence tests skewed in favor of middle-class children, but also of the middle-class school system.

Spiker and McCandless hold that favoring or disfavoring middle-class schools is not a scientific evaluation: "science cannot tell us what the 'better' life is." They also think it important that existing

[26]Gustav Bergmann: The logic of psychological concepts, *Philosophy of Science, 18,* 1951.

[27]Kenneth Eells, Allison Davis, Robert S. Havighurst, Virgil E. Herrick and Ralph Tyler: *Intelligence and Cultural Differences,* Chicago, University of Chicago Press, 1951, especially Ch. XXII. Also of interest, and summarizing more recent work, is Frank Riessman: *The Culturally Deprived Child,* New York, Harper & Row, 1962, Ch. VI.

tests do have predictive value (but are careful not to overestimate that value), and argue that if those tests predict success in middle-class schools, it is pointless to want them to predict something else, such as success in less socially stratified schools.

The present writer agrees that some of the literature on culture-free tests is confused and shows only too clearly the ideological preferences of the authors. On the other hand, Spiker and Mc-candless' dismissal seems too easy; fairly important questions are involved.

Although one may agree with Spiker and McCandless that at least some connotations of ordinary language terms can be "left out" when terms are put to technical uses, there is plenty of room here for confusion, both on the part of the expert and on the part of the layman. If someone thought of intelligence as general problem solving ability, and then was told that middle-class children score higher than lower-class children on intelligence tests, he presumably would draw the obvious conclusion. And yet the test may be doing no more than predicting school success fairly well. If some tests purporting to measure clerical aptitude (as apparently is the case) do not predict what nearly all of us would regard as success in clerical functions, and in fact predict some nonclerical aptitudes, we may be pardoned for thinking the test is misnamed.[28] Although not all ordinary language connotations need be taken account of, then, if what is measured is poorly described by the terminology used, the sensible procedure would be to change the terminology.

The "culture-free" test developers also think that many people may not be aware that middle-class preference systems in fact dominate many schools. The assumption that all classes share the same basic outlook, or that schools are neutral toward class differences, apparently is very much mistaken. What those developers may be objecting to is not that existing tests predict what they do predict, but rather that they are often assumed to predict something else. Using the Spiker-McCandless terminology, many "factual" as well as "value" issues are involved, and one can be critical of certain widely used tests without introducing "values."

---

[28]See Edward E. Cureton: Validity, in E. F. Lindquist, ed.: *Educational Measurement*, Washington, D. C., American Council on Education, 1951, p. 621.

3. DIAGNOSIS OF SOME TYPES OF TERMINOLOGICAL PROBLEMS

a) Fairly often in the behavioral sciences, problems arise because a term having many connotations in ordinary language is specified much more narrowly for scientific purposes. In the previous section, "intelligence," "information," "rationality," and "control" are examples. As emphasized earlier, not only laymen but sometimes the experts then leap to the conclusion that notions previously vague, confused, inconsistent, etc., now have been clarified, and that what once was speculative is now scientific. To take an extremely crude and artificial example, if one "operationally defined" the term "religious" solely in terms of a certain frequency of church attendance, he might have a tightly controlled inquiry, but we would be entitled to be suspicious of the results in terms of phenomena generally thought to be religious.

Considerable attention has been given to this problem in the present chapter because it seems related to many important issues, including both some much heralded "breakthroughs" and some bitter denunciations of behavioral science in general. Behavioral scientists often face something of a dilemma. If an ordinary language term is used inconsistently, or in very many ways, or if it seems to postulate dubious entities, any restricted technical specification may give rise to charges "but that's not what we mean by ...." On the other hand, if a new technical term is introduced to replace the common sense one, the relevance of the inquiry may be obscured. The problem, as stated so far, of course is not peculiar to the behavioral sciences; physicists had the same problem with "force" and other words. The situation is exacerbated in the behavioral areas because the practitioners themselves often are confused as to what they are doing. The absence of a generally agreed upon terminology for use across the behavioral fields also leads to communication difficulties. In general the situation seems to call for greater emphasis on developing suitable nomenclature, more attention to what is being inquired into, and a higher degree of skepticism than is commonly exhibited about the present success of communication.

b) Sometimes there are either no observable referents for terms used, or the formal definitions of the terms seem inconsistent with what can be observed. Many accounts of "utility," "rationality," and "sovereignty" seem to fall into this difficulty. What is helpful in developing a plausible theory may unfortunately not refer to any aspect of human behavior, but the delights of the theory may still incline people to hunt snarks.

c) Sometimes there are not only identifiable referents, but apparently a very high agreement among objective investigators in locating those referents, yet there is disagreement or unclarity about specifying the term. "Morpheme" and "culture" seem to be examples of this. The difficulty may be minor, but it also may be symptomatic of mistaken assumptions about human behavior.

d) Although vagueness and ambiguity are always possible dangers, the use of some terms is especially prone to those dangers. In the preceding section, "value" seems to be a prime example.

e) Sometimes the "level of reality" referred to is a subject of controversy, as in the case of "culture." Since "reality" is such a troublesome word, it is not always possible to discern exactly what is being argued about, but at least in some instances disputes involve the proper methods and techniques to be used in the inquiry. Although contemporary behavioral scientists seem very alert to the dangers of reification, it is still sometimes indulged in unwittingly. The hope of "carving out" an autonomous, or at least relatively distinct, area of inquiry may lead workers to engage in a type of verbal magic that impedes rather than helps inquiry into the relevant aspects of human behavior.

f) Sometimes the terminology used leads to the evasion of actual problems of human behavior and the substitution of problems generated by particular theoretical systems. Some ways of differentiating "sovereignty" from observable governmental processes, and some attempts to measure "utility," illustrate what is intended here.

4. COMPARISON WITH PHYSICAL SCIENCE TERMINOLOGY

The relative importance of terminological disputes and confusions seems much less in the physical sciences than in the behavioral disciplines. This is not to say, of course, that all is well in the natural sciences. For example, some physicists tended to cling to the reality of "ether" after the supposed effects of that entity proved to be unobservable. But at least compared to other scientific areas, the terminology used in the physical sciences either has empirical referents or is linked to such referents.

Anatol Rapoport has discussed this issue.[29] He says that for physicists, "concepts come as natural by-products of observing certain regularities inherent in relations among measurable quantities." For example, the amount of electric current in a wire is found to be proportional to the potential difference impressed, and the constant of proportionality is named "coefficient of resistance." Rapoport goes on to describe the physicist as "predominantly occupied with uncovering objectively identifiable and consistent regularities."

However, he maintains that the social scientist's "concepts"[30] are more difficult to achieve than the physical scientist's, for the social scientist often does not measure, but rather abstracts from observation. He goes on:

"The physicist's concepts make sense only if everyone gets the same results from measurements under identical conditions. Similarly, the social scientist's concepts make sense if everyone recognizes the same situations as identical and makes the same abstractions from similar observations."

Rapoport thinks a start has been made, through the use of mathematical models, in building a social science comparable to natural science developments.

In the present writer's opinion, many behavioral science inquiries do proceed along the lines Rapoport attributes to the physical scientists, but not necessarily by means of mathematical models. It may be observed that the terminology of the natural scientists causes comparatively little difficulty just because "everyone gets the same results from measurements under identical conditions," and the nomenclature is directly linked to those measurements. The institutionalization of controls to eliminate subjectivity, bias, etc.,

[29]Anatol Rapoport: Uses and limitations of mathematical models in social sciences, in Llewellyn Gross, ed.: *Symposium on Sociological Theory*, Evanston, Row, Peterson, 1959. All quotations given here are from p. 352.

[30]The heavy use of "concept" often carries with it many difficulties; perhaps it and "meaning" are best not used. For problems of the use of "concept" in physics, see: Physicists and fairies, Ch. 7, of Arthur F. Bentley: *Inquiry into Inquiries*, Boston, Beacon Press, 1954.

also plays an important role in the physical sciences. If the natural sciences had developed without that institutionalization, then they might well have occupied a position similar to that which the behavioral sciences now occupy.

Finally, it should be emphasized again that much of the material of interest to behavioral scientists concerns the use of signs. The notorious capacities of humans to get tangled in their verbalizations leads to special difficulties here, since that entanglement is involved in both the materials to be investigated and the investigative techniques.

5. CONCLUDING COMMENTARY

According to George A. Lundberg:

"Man has always stood in awe of his verbalizations, especially when they are in written form and are traceable to ancient sources. No feeling is more widespread than that the structure of our language, that most fundamental repository of our culture, *must* represent, and closely correspond to, the structure and nature of reality. When, therefore, we find deeply engrained in our language different types of sentence structure, we are sure that the phenomena, the events, or the processes these sentences purport to describe are fundamentally of a different order."[31]

The comments just quoted perhaps would be accepted by a great many behavioral scientists, but certainly powerful philosophic and other intellectual currents oppose what Lundberg says. To mention only one example, in his recent study of "free action," A. I. Melden sees highly important differences between the language of natural events and the language of human conduct. He puts considerable emphasis on the difference between describing an arm as "rising" and as "being raised," and draws some of his major conclusions from the differences in the two types of language.[32]

In the present writer's opinion, much of the difficulty in contemporary behavioral inquiries stems from terminological problems. Those problems in turn stem partly from the awe of verbalization that Lundberg mentions. A major attempt to clarify that terminology is advocated here, on the grounds that existing terminology often hampers inquiry.

[31]George A. Lundberg: Semantics and the value problem, *Social Forces*, 27:114, 1948.
[32]A. I. Melden: *Free Action*, London, Routledge & Kegan Paul, 1961.

Indeed, one reason so much jargon creeps into behavioral science discussions may be the underlying notion that man's verbal behavior is so important, significant, and cosmically rare that a highly elaborate theoretical structure must be necessary to explain it. This, of course, is not to deny the high degree of complexity that characterizes much human behavior, but is a caution that we should not always assume that everything is of great difficulty. Behavioral inquiries into the highly complex forms of human activity are sometimes successful. (From reading certain discussions of humans altering their behavior in view of predictions made about that behavior, one might assume that successful predictions are hardly ever made.)

Although objections are made in this monograph to needlessly complex terminology, no claim is made here that ordinary language will suffice or even that ordinary language is modified only at great peril. The view here is that terminology having a clear use in inquiry should be emphasized. If inquiry shows that ordinary language connotations should be discarded, then that is what should be done. If we succeed in accurately predicting human behavior, we need not worry particularly about what changes may have been made in common sense language. The danger, of course, as mentioned earlier, is that we sometimes think we have measured something corresponding to ordinary language usage, when in fact something very different has been investigated. To revert to an earlier example, if what we want to predict is problem solving ability in a variety of situations, and the test used in fact predicts success in a certain type of school situation, we have a possible confusion. But if we are clear as to what we want to predict, then the labels we use may not be too important, so long as they do not lead ourselves or others to mistake what has been done.

In short, the thesis of this chapter is that problems of terminology and nomenclature are often more important than behavioral scientists believe. The criterion for importance here is not some pedantic philosophic inclination, but rather concerns the extent to which present terminology tends to hinder the development of warranted assertions about human action.[33]

---

[33]For a discussion of terminological problems in specific scientific disciplines, see Section 6 of each chapter of Rollo Handy and Paul Kurtz: *A Current Appraisal of the Behavioral Sciences*, Great Barrington, Mass., Behavioral Research Council, 1964. Some of the materials of the present chapter are adapted from that volume.

9

PROSPECTS, PROBLEMS, AND CONCLUSION

1. GENERAL POINT OF VIEW

OFTEN people who argue that behavioral inquiries, in principle, can be fully scientific maintain also that many results of major significance have already been achieved. Those holding that scientific method is only partially applicable to human behavior frequently argue that not much has been accomplished. The view in this monograph combines a highly optimistic outlook for the future of scientific inquiries into the problems of men in society with a fairly negative opinion of the results achieved to date. It is perhaps only to be expected that behavioral scientists tend to exaggerate the merits and the range of application of what they have achieved, and their overexuberance may be a factor in the critics' dim appraisal of the potentialities of a hard science approach. Since preceding chapters have been concerned with showing that the alleged methodological limitations of such an approach are often incorrect, attention now will be given to a review of some reasons that more has not been accomplished.

2. MAJOR OBSTACLES

Neither the supposed greater difficulty and complexity of behavioral problems, nor related methodological complications, can account fully for the failures of behavioral scientists to achieve more than they have. As discussed previously, two factors may be singled out as among the major handicaps. The first concerns the belief, widespread in our culture, of the very special nature of human activity when compared to other cosmic processes. This belief can be crude or sophisticated, and may involve a sharp dualism between mind and matter, emphasize the uniqueness of man's symbolic behavior, or otherwise uphold a highly privileged status

for man. The assumption is often made that since man is so special
the general way of inquiring into other aspects of nature cannot be
applied to him, or else must be supplemented with a variety of
techniques supposedly more appropriate to the subject matter.

The second major obstacle relates to the way the disciplines
studying man have been institutionalized in our culture. The weakness of a scientific tradition in the study of man, the allocation of
prestige on bases other than scientific achievement, and the custom
of judging hypotheses primarily as to their plausibility within some
nonscientific framework, seem to be significant factors here. The
relatively large gap between the work of the theoretician and the
laboratorian has been especially detrimental. Neither overt arguments that some statements about human behavior can be accepted
on a nonempirical basis, nor arguments that theory should be
eschewed, are as dangerous in this context as the emphasis in
official methodological statements on the testing of hypotheses combined with relatively little concern shown for such testing in practice.

3. SOME OTHER HINDRANCES TO BEHAVIORAL INQUIRY

Humans, when blocked in the pursuit of some activity, are ingenious in finding substitutes that offer considerable satisfaction.
Some situations occuring both in behavioral inquiry and in methodological discussions about inquiry suggest that kind of substitution, for often the primary urge of the inquirer is frustrated. He
may lack financial resources for studying what he wants; he may
lack the relevant information necessary to develop hypotheses
worthy of testing; or there may be sociocultural obstacles to his
investigation. Under such circumstances, it can be tempting indeed
to turn to theoretical considerations that are almost totally removed
from anything going on in inquiry. It is hard not to believe that
there is sometimes too much technical discussion of certain matters
along with a neglect of much more important issues. At its worst,
such technical talk is even pseudo-technical, for there is no reason
or use for it except the prestige flowing from the manipulation of
symbols. At other times, the level of technicality far outruns a sober
consideration of other, prior, matters.

For example, models that have not been shown to have any relevance at all for human behavior may be developed to an astoundingly high degree, until only a few experts can follow the technical discussions of their structure and interrelations. Such theoretical productions can develop enormous internal momentum. Great intelligence is needed to elaborate and "fill out" the details, and a sizable literature can grow up around the topic. Yet practically no attention may be given to whether the model is of the slightest aid in predicting, explaining, understanding, or otherwise describing human behavior. Some accounts of rational behavior, for example, have a beautiful internal structure, but the care lavished on that structure may be paralleled by cavalier statements about its relation to the human behavior it was designed to illuminate.

Another problem concerns lack of communication among workers in various behavioral areas. Frequently similar endeavors go on in different academic fields, but apparently little or no interchange among the investigators occurs. Different sets of terminology may be developed, which can further exacerbate the problem of communication. And since often inquiry has been institutionalized so that prestige within the discipline matters more than other kinds of prestige, we find that interdisciplinary efforts are often given an honorific place verbally, but that actual research is concentrated on what can be done within conventional disciplinary lines.

Tensions between in-groups and out-groups also occur. Sadly enough, the views of a person from another discipline are often evaluated, not in terms of possible contributions to empirical problems, but in terms of the mastery of the accepted jargon. If problems came neatly divided along conventional disciplinary lines, there would be more reason to be suspicious of "outsiders," for they might lack the training, information, and skills necessary to make significant contributions. But the disciplinary lines seem very poorly organized in terms of the problems to be solved in studying human behavior. The great pains taken to assure everyone that a given problem belongs to a particular discipline can afford considerable amusement. On the one hand, imperialistic tendencies in specifying the range of a discipline are sometimes prominent, and each discipline ends up laying claim to all human behavior, or nearly so.

When that approach seems too questionable, another often is sub-stituted. The inquirer is interested in certain aspects of human be-havior, but to show that he is, say, a proper political scientist, he may differentiate the political aspect from the social, economic, psychological, cultural, etc., until the result is ludicrous. The tradi-tions of a discipline, then, may be much more influential on what is studied, and how, than considerations of the best techniques to facilitate the development of relevant warranted assertions.

Finally, looking at workers in behavioral fields in general, there seems to be no doubt that many of the most intelligent, devoted, and influential people either oppose a fully scientific approach or feel that such an approach has grave limitations. In some disciplines, only a few people urge a scientific approach. Possible reasons for this have already been discussed. When most of the highly capable people in a discipline are skeptical of the merits of scientific inquiry, we may expect their influence to be considerable for some time to come.

4. INCONCLUSIVENESS OF MANY ARGUMENTS

As noted earlier, methodological discussions often become quite sterile. Attention is drawn here to the importance of varying no-tions of scientific method. Although agreement may occur about the words used to formulate the key aspects of that method, the way those words are understood operationally may help perpetuate con-troversies. Perhaps the best example is that of highly mathematical models. Those adopting a view of science verbally similar to the one urged here may exhibit a wide range of opinions about the useful-ness of those models. Frequently all participants in the debate agree that as yet the prediction of actual behavior has not been aided by the models, and yet the model-builders' confidence is not dimin-ished. The proponents of models tend to see existing models as the first step in the development of more satisfactory ones; their op-ponents emphasize present deficiencies. Implicit in many of these disagreements seem to be conflicting views as to the extent theories and testing should be linked. We need to cut beneath mere verbal agreement to see what assumptions actually are operative.

Central, therefore, to all major themes of this monograph is the question of what is taken as constituting scientific method.

5. PRESENT APPROACH TO SCIENTIFIC METHOD

In outline, the following approach for arriving at a specification of "scientific method" is advocated.

We begin with those forms of human behavior commonly designated scientific. It is not surprising to find that many inconsistent practices are so designated, and that we find variation historically, across disciplinary lines, and within disciplines in any one time period. Although some inquiries have been much more successful than others, we find differing criteria of success. Even when the same notion of success is adopted, there are sometimes differences of opinion as to how much was achieved.

There then seems to be no reasonable alternative to what in one sense is an arbitrary approach; that is, singling out from the various activities labeled "science" just what will be taken as central. Development of a working set of rules for differentiating science from nonscience was undertaken in earlier chapters. Using those rules, it is possible to rate, at least roughly, the scientific merit of various activities going by the name scientific inquiry. The postulation adopted stresses prediction, control (or appropriate adjustive behavior when control is impossible), and intersubjective agreement through empirical testing. Those who prefer other tests often can be found, especially if judged by their full behavior rather than merely by their "official" utterances. Persistent differences among such preferences help to account for the unsatisfactory nature of some controversies.

The success in facilitating prediction and control in the physical sciences when certain procedures were developed underlies the hope in this volume that similar results will follow when parallel procedures are followed in the investigation of human behavior. Some impressive results in the latter investigations can be cited, but primary reliance here has been on the weakness of alleged arguments against the possibility of such results. Showing that such arguments are weak does not, of course, provide satisfactory evidence that success will be forthcoming, but it may clear away some of the hindrances to the vigorous pursuit of scientific inquiry.

6. TYPES OF THEORY OF THE BEHAVIORAL SCIENCES

Relatively little attention has been given to a taxonomy of contemporary types of theory of the behavioral sciences. The four
patterns discussed by May Brodbeck will help to illustrate some of
the points made above.[1] She differentiates: (1) The "self-conscious
continuers of the Galilean-Newtonian tradition," who argue for the
same method in the behavioral as in the physical areas of inquiry
and frequently maintain that the social is somehow reducible to the
psychological, which is reducible to the physiological, which in
turn is reducible to the physical; (2) The romantics, who emphasize
organic, holistic, and emergentist notions, insist that the sciences of
man are unique, and often criticize the physical science view as
"viciously demeaning to the dignity of man and his works"; (3)
Some Marxists and pragmatists, who urge an objective and scientific study of social phenomena, but who maintain that social
"laws" are unique in kind and not assimilable to psychological or
physical laws; and (4) Those sometimes calling themselves methodological individualists, who maintain that group behavior is reducible to the behavior of individuals, but that the "psychology of
individuals cannot be reduced to anything else."

Brodbeck goes on to make the important point that frequently
those debating the above questions are not aware that they are
trying to anticipate the results of future scientific research. They
tend to make assertions about what they think *must* occur, and in
that sense prematurely foreclose inquiry.

Discussions of reducibility of "laws" are frequently inconclusive
and unsatisfactory, and when the "laws" in question have not
yet been discovered, we may find it more fruitful to direct our
energies elsewhere. It is bad enough to discuss whether *all* "laws"
can be reduced to those of physics, but when we have hardly any
social "laws" in the first place, we can hardly expect much illumina-
tion from the debates.

Using the four patterns discussed by Brodbeck, the point of view
presented in this monograph can be clarified. An attempt is made

---

[1]May Brodbeck: On the philosophy of the social sciences, *Philosophy of Science*, 21:
1954. Quotations cited in this section are from pp. 140-41.

here to unite elements of her first two patterns, but not along the lines of either the third or fourth patterns. To postulate in advance either reducibility or nonreducibility seems pointless and indeed often detrimental to inquiry. Rather the needs of a specific inquiry should be paramount. We strive to develop warranted assertions about certain behavior. In some cases, that development may be facilitated by looking for the "atoms" making up the behavior. At other times, however, concentrating attention on the relations of the "atoms" to each other and to other things, may be more important. The "reductionists" often have the great merit of insisting on hard science methods, but they also often have the defect of arbitrarily isolating and separating what is best studied in a more holistic context.

Closely related is the question of whether priority should be given to the "burning issues" or to less important matters that can be handled rigorously with available techniques. Too often in recent behavioral science a split has occurred between those who use excellent scientific methods, but on peripheral or unimportant materials, and those who work on important problems but with lamentable methods. As discussed earlier, the stand taken here was for pursuing the burning issues, but using hard science methods.

To avoid one possible misunderstanding, there is no emotional or ideological bias here against reductionism. The present author would be pleased if in fact it turned out that all behavior can be described and explained solely in physical terms. He also sees no threat to human dignity in such reduction and denies that man would be thereby demeaned. But to date, at least, the specific kind of inquiries successful in physics do not seem applicable to much of human behavior, whereas some other techniques have resulted in at least some gains. Progress in predicting voting behavior, for example, has come not through a study of the atomic structure of voters, but in quite different ways. Therefore, what is urged here is that energies be devoted to whatever promises, in a particular context of inquiry, to yield warranted assertions. As argued earlier, even when in some clear sense one kind of behavior is reducible to another, inquiry may be carried out most efficiently without bothering about the reduction.[2]

---

[2]See Chapter III, Section 1.

7. CONCLUDING SUMMARY

In many respects the position taken here either falls between more extreme positions found in the literature, or supports views that are not very popular. To avoid misunderstanding as much as possible, it may be helpful to conclude with a summary of the general position adopted and an indication of the lines of support for that position.

(a) In contrast to many current approaches, no sharp differentiation is made between *philosophical* and *scientific, conceptual* and *empirical,* or *methodological* and *substantive* problems. For rough and ready general purposes, or within specific contexts, such distinctions can be useful. But all of those factors may be involved in the discovery of warranted assertions about human behavior, and sharp differentiation of them may lead to misunderstanding of the behavior. Often disagreements occur about what constitutes knowing and about the relation of knower and known, thus linking so-called philosophic and scientific problems. The hypotheses used in inquiry are bound to what "facts" are found, and the assumed "facts" influence the further development of hypotheses, thus linking the conceptual and the empirical. What are regarded as substantive problems may be highly dependent on the methodology adopted, as in disagreements as to how satisfactory motive explanations are. The unraveling of what goes on in inquiry, then, may best be facilitated by ignoring some of the conventional distinctions and divisions of labor.

In the same vein, many distinctions between *pure* and *applied* science are here rejected. In an obvious sense, a distinction can be made between a warranted "if-then" assertion and its application to the solution of some problem. But theoretical and applied problems are often only artificially separable. The search for an answer to a "practical" problem may lead to new "theoretical" findings. Supposed "disinterested" curiosity may be as potent in solving an engineering problem as in solving a "pure" problem. What is basic and what is applied, what is pure and what is practical, need to be specified within the context of particular inquiries.

(b) Philosophers of science often are not very aware of behavioral science literature, and even more important, of the assumptions and working framework of those scientists. Philosophers are prone to fixate on words, or on final reports of an inquiry, rather than on the full process. To grasp what is involved in scientific inquiry leads into many areas other than the logical structure of arguments. However important that structure may be, other aspects of scientific inquiry are also important.[3]

(c) The advocacy here of hard science techniques stems from the successes of those techniques in natural science investigations. Of course it is admitted that if human behavior were radically different from natural phenomena, some other model of inquiry might be necessary. But the defenses of a different mode of inquiry seem to flow primarily from a prior commitment to a difference between man and nature, not from the failures of scientific inquiry into human affairs. The case for a hard science approach would be more impressive if greater results had already been achieved, but again the opponents of that approach often seem to be poorly acquainted with what has been accomplished, especially as compared to the results of nonscientific approaches. Judgments obviously will differ, but I think the present situation in regard to the possibilities of a scientific attack on human behavior is similar to that prevailing before the common acceptance of a scientific attack on natural science problems.

Very likely there will always be people who find scientific achievements boring, or trivial, or lacking in humanistic significance. All that is advocated here is that if the kind of prediction and control typical of scientific inquiry is wanted, then surely of all ways of knowing that man has tried, the scientific offers most grounds for success. What we find, at least sometimes, are those who want that prediction and control, but look for some short cut way to get it. When faced with difficulties of crisis proportions, humans often desire a solution they can accept totally. The age old quest for certainty has enormous attraction for many today. Humans exhibit great potential for allowing momentous decisions to be made on flimsy evidence.

In view of the failures of other methods of inquiry, however, it seems that only scientific inquiry offers any realistic hope of solving

---

[3]Mario Bunge, for example, has argued that the "*methodological* status of the predicate basis is, then, far more important than its logical structure and number." See Ch. 7 of his *The Myth of Simplicity*, Englewood Cliffs, N. J., Prentice-Hall, 1963.

our major problems. Yet considering the relative lack of basic research in human relations, we may have to wait for a long time to get results that will withstand the requisite tests and solve our problems. Until then, partial solutions and helpful data may become available. One suspects that sometimes the commitment to nonscientific modes of inquiry stems in part from unwillingness to wait for adequate answers.

(d) The advocacy of hard science techniques within a holistic frame of reference, here called transactionalism, is urged because the highly atomistic, analytic views often fail to work well, and the conditions of inquiry force us to take a more holistic position. Economists sometimes hamper their own efforts, for example, by relying on crude psychological assumptions, or ignoring cultural differences. Psychologists and political scientists often overgeneralize in projecting adequate descriptions of the behavior of *some* humans on all humanity. This of course is not to oppose concentration on certain restricted aspects of a transaction, for that may be extremely useful, but rather to point out that such concentration may be mistaken for a full account of the behaviors involved, or lead to neglect of important variables.

(e) The kind of relation urged between the work of the theoretician and the laboratorian also flows from an analysis of what goes on in successful inquiry, and is emphatically not hostile to theory. However, the prominence in many behavioral disciplines of elaborate theoretical structures that are untested and sometimes well-nigh untestable leads here to criticism that might be misunderstood as anti-theoretical. But criticism of some speculative efforts is balanced by criticism of those who may not be aware of how theoretical some of their "findings" are. The sharp differentiation sometimes made between *facts* and *interpretation* may have pernicious results, especially if it is supposed that there are no problems about the facts but only about the interpretation of them.

Some of the discussions about "burning issues" versus researchable problems may also be viewed in the present context. A difficulty with some "burning issues" is not that they are too complex to be handled scientifically, but that disagreements about them have not been linked to empirical data that are either already available or could be gathered. A concerted attack on such problems using hard science techniques might well produce many solutions. In short, both theory and data collection, "big" problems and hard techniques, are supported here, instead of a commitment to one part of supposed polar extremes.

(f) Implicit in some accounts of scientific method is a kind of architectural view that is here opposed. Some proceed as if science develops in layers, so to speak, in which cumulative additions to the store of facts are made, and theories erected on the basis of those facts. Although something like this indeed happens, the over-simplification involved can be dangerous. The naivete of assuming there is a pure given in perception, or that we have adequate knowledge of hard facts upon which we can base our theories, seems to be carried over into methodological discussions, with the result that critical scrutiny and constant checking and rechecking of both data and theory are ignored or insufficiently emphasized. When theoretical and laboratory work are related in the manner here suggested, we seem to have maximum opportunity to correct assumed facts in view of well-supported generalizations, and in a position to spend minimal time on hypotheses badly out of accord with experimental findings. The methodology used should be as much under the control of well-established findings as future research is under the control of methodology.[4]

(g) The stress on terminological problems throughout this book needs to be distinguished from certain other emphases current in philosophy, especially those in some analytic movements. The major line of differentiation is that here any sharp separation of sign from sign-user is deplored. The handling of words as if they had a life of their own can lead to many peculiar results.

Some current views adopt a threefold distinction between semantics, syntactics, and pragmatics. The present view, in contrast, regards that distinction as often misleading. All three areas are of considerable concern in inquiry into inquiry, and the tendency to ignore pragmatics is a grievous fault of certain contemporary accounts of scientific method. The focus in this volume has been on those terms that seem to hamper inquiry rather than facilitate it.

---

[4]This point of view has been elaborated by the present author: Personality factors and intellectual production, *Philosophy of Science*, *23*, 1956; Philosophy's neglect of the social sciences, *Philosophy of Science*, *25*, 1958; and Some possible contributions of sociology to philosophy, *Sociology and Social Research*, *48*, 1964.

Such terms may offer few, if any problems, on the "levels" of syntax or semantics, but can become major problems on the "level" of pragmatics. A formally unobjectionable definition, for example, may impede inquiry if the assumptions leading to that definition are badly out of accord with relatively well-established findings about human behavior. On the other hand, what might cause raised eyebrows in terms of formal definition, etc., might function well in actual inquiry. Terminology given a clean bill of health from a particular philosophic perspective may produce great problems in empirical inquiry, while terminology that philosophers are suspicious of may facilitate that inquiry. Terminological problems, then, are best viewed in the context of inquiry.

(h) In terms of basic scientific method, no difference is admitted here between the natural and the behavioral sciences. How one views this issue, of course, is dependent on what is meant by "basic." The position developed in the first three chapters indicates what is intended here. But along with an insistence on a "hard," "natural," or "full" science approach goes a tolerant, permissive attitude toward the specific techniques, types of hypotheses, and methods of manipulating data that are considered admissible. Whatever can be handled in conformity with the empirical testing of hypotheses is allowed; there is no attempt to draw up a list of proper procedures that apply universally. Specifically, the view in this book should not be confused with any contemporary view taking physics as *the* science and urging that workers in other disciplines do just as the physicists do. The wilder psychoanalytic speculations can be opposed, for example, without insisting that human sign-behavior be studied in the physics laboratory.

In some respects, physics does not seem a desirable model for the behavioral sciences. For one thing, the extreme emphasis on axiomatic deductive systems in some phases of physical research may offer only too much encouragement to certain behavioral workers, who lack the great body of warranted assertions available for the development and testing of axiomatic systems in physics. The specific techniques, terminology, and ways of controlling variables in physics are often not useful in behavioral areas. But physics is a desirable model viewed in terms of the kind of prediction, control, intersubjective agreement, etc., often achieved there.

(i) The usefulness of quantification in many scientific areas is so great that it should be made clear that no hostility is intended toward quantification and the heavy use of mathematics in the behavioral sciences. What was opposed is the attempt to by-pass crucial problems of testing in favor of the elaboration of formal structures, and the assurance some exhibit that tight control exercised over such symbolic structures will necessarily result in great benefits for the prediction and control of human behavior. Especially pernicious in certain aspects of behavioral investigation is the translation into mathematical symbolism of extremely dubious notions, followed by the manipulation of the symbols, and the re-translation of the results back into conventional language, all with an air of great accomplishment. If the original data were unsound, nothing but mystification may be gained from such transformations of it.

No patience is shown here for those who propound obscurantist notions about intrinsically unquantifiable phenomena, or who cavalierly attempt to rise above "mere" counting and precise measurement. But at the same time, there seems to be no point in rejecting some procedures as unscientific merely because they are not quantified to the extent we might desire. On occasion even the prediction of the *direction of change* of a variable may be quite an accomplishment, and humanly very significant, even if we wish a more precise prediction of the *magnitude* of the change were possible.

In the nine summarizing points above, the emphasis has been on inquiry into inquiry, and the conclusions drawn are those that seem warranted by an analysis of successful inquiries, with success being judged in terms of prediction, control, intersubjective agreement, etc. But no attempt has been made to set down final or unchangeable methodological canons. As more inquiries are made, some changes in methodological commentary on those inquiries probably will be called for, including possible rejection of what previously seemed sound. Constant reference has been made to the context of inquiry, since other observers may have different criteria by which they judge various investigations.

The study of human behavior is often fascinating, especially the responses made to other people's sign-behavior, and our further responses to our own verbalizations. To make that study scientific, not only in intent but in practice, is a formidable challenge. Human ingenuity in showing the "impossibility" of such scientific inquiry is also fascinating. A basic theme of this book has been that there are no apparent theoretical obstacles to such inquiry, but there are more than enough other obstacles to keep a great many scientists busy for a long time.

INDEX

177